PARENTING WITH FIRE

Lighting Up the Family
with Passion and Inspiration

SHMULEY BOTEACH

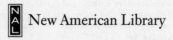 New American Library

New American Library
Published by New American Library, a division of
Penguin Group (USA) Inc., 375 Hudson Street,
New York, New York 10014, USA
Penguin Group (Canada), 90 Eglinton Avenue East, Suite 700, Toronto,
Ontario M4P 2Y3, Canada (a division of Pearson Penguin Canada Inc.)
Penguin Books Ltd., 80 Strand, London WC2R 0RL, England
Penguin Ireland, 25 St. Stephen's Green, Dublin 2,
Ireland (a division of Penguin Books Ltd.)
Penguin Group (Australia), 250 Camberwell Road, Camberwell, Victoria 3124,
Australia (a division of Pearson Australia Group Pty. Ltd.)
Penguin Books India Pvt. Ltd., 11 Community Centre, Panchsheel Park,
New Delhi - 110 017, India
Penguin Group (NZ), cnr Airborne and Rosedale Roads, Albany,
Auckland 1310, New Zealand (a division of Pearson New Zealand Ltd.)
Penguin Books (South Africa) (Pty.) Ltd., 24 Sturdee Avenue,
Rosebank, Johannesburg 2196, South Africa

Penguin Books Ltd., Registered Offices:
80 Strand, London WC2R 0RL, England

First published by New American Library,
a division of Penguin Group (USA) Inc.

First Printing, September 2006
10 9 8 7 6 5 4 3 2

N
A
L   REGISTERED TRADEMARK—MARCA REGISTRADA

LIBRARY OF CONGRESS CATALOGING-IN-PUBLICATION DATA

Boteach, Shmuley.
   Parenting with fire: lighting up the family with passion and inspiration/Shmuley
Boteach.
      p. cm.
   ISBN 0-451-21977-5
   1. Child rearing—Religious aspects—Judaism. 2. Child rearing—United States.
3. Parenting—Religious aspects—Judaism. 4. Jewish families—United States—Religious
life. 5. Jewish religious education of children—United States. I. Title.
   HQ769.3.B68 2006
   296.7'4—dc22   2006010260

Set in Janson Text
Designed by Spring Hoteling

Printed in the United States of America

To the memory of my grandmother, Eshrat, who
loved me and inspired me. A mother of thirteen and
grandmother to scores more, she taught me that
family is life's foremost blessing.
And to my parents-in-law, Sam and Eva,
who gave me my wife, Debbie.

Acknowledgements

First and foremost, I wish to thank Laura Tucker, who has now worked with me on three books. Laura is a brilliant woman, writer, and editor, but her greatest role, and the one she excels at most, is Mom. I have grown wiser from Laura's questions and insights, and remain profoundly indebted to her.

My parents gave me my core values, and if there is good in me, then they deserve the principal thanks. More than anything else, they taught me to love G-d and to love all G-d's children. Life has no higher lesson.

My brothers and sisters are, and have always been, my closest confidants and the people who, along with my wife, know me best and around whom I can act with no pretense. They are much better siblings to me than I am to them. But as I'm the youngest, they have always indulged me, so I will continue to assert my right to be spoiled.

My wife is the person I respect most in the world. She is pure goodness and there isn't a day that goes by that she doesn't inspire me to be a better human being, more patient, more compassionate, more understanding. Being married to her humbles me.

My children are the light of my life and the source of my greatest happiness. All it takes is for me to just think of them to be happy. G-d, it's a beautiful thing to be a parent. And speaking of G-d, thank you, O Lord of heaven and earth, for the infinite blessings you have always given me, none greater than a loving family with whom to share my life. I pray that I will always prove worthy of G-d's love.

The Lubavitcher Rebbe, Rabbi Menachem Schneerson, of blessed memory, was the greatest man I ever met, and it was due to his inspiration that I became a rabbi, met my wife, and had eight children. I miss him every day.

Contents

CONTENTS

Love

Activity

CONTENTS

NOVELTY

TRADITION

CONCLUSION

PARENTING
WITH FIRE

INTRODUCTION

Fanning the Flames Within:
Parenting—and Living—with Fire

> There are only two lasting bequests
> we can hope to give our children.
> One is roots; the other, wings.
> —Hodding Carter

As host of the TLC show *Shalom in the Home*, I've traveled across the United States, and I've seen the same story unfolding in home after home. You're doing everything "right"—you love your kids, you give them structure, discipline, the best education and guidance you can provide. But you're not seeing any return on your investment of time and effort. Instead, your family is falling apart: your children are unruly, rebellious, and uncommunicative. They sulk like zombies, offering monosyllables in response to questions; they don't live in the home so much as haunt it, and the only time they come to life is when they're with their friends. You have to bribe them to get them to do the simplest thing, and they don't seem to internalize any of the direction you give them, leaving you feeling not like a voice of authority but like a nag.

And that's the best-case scenario! Many parents these days find themselves held hostage by children who are downright abusive, who cut themselves, who experiment with sex and drugs. And the children themselves seem miserable. They feel misunderstood, unloved—and in many cases they're putting themselves in very real danger, whether it's from adult sexual predators, sexually transmitted diseases, or drug overdose.

All these behavioral problems, as disparate as they may seem on the surface, fall under one umbrella. They are all symptoms of a single disease, and the diagnosis is right in front of our noses: **Childhood is the great casualty of modern-day living.**

All around us, we are producing a generation of kids who simply have not had the joy, who have not been accorded the right, who have not been allowed the freedom of *knowing what it's like to be a kid.*

Where is the peace in the lives of our children? And without it, how will they ever know confidence? Where is the security in the lives of our children? Without it, how will they ever know serenity? Where is the joy in the lives of our children? Without it, how will they ever know bliss? Enveloped as they are by the noise of a culture that seeks to eradicate everything childlike and innocent about them, silenced by neglect, and enraged by abandonment, can we really say that there are any children left in America?

And our children aren't the only ones who suffer as a result of this anger and lack of inspiration; their parents show wounds as well. After all, our home is supposed to be a place of solace, of comfort—a haven where we can rest and recharge, not a battlefield. Our families are supposed to provide us with a sense of contentment, strength, support, and pride—they're not supposed to be stressors that we escape to the office to avoid! But I hear over and over again that parents themselves have had it with the endless battles, the nagging and the disrespect. And so, worn down and wrung out, they've thrown in the towel, capitulating in the face of their children's insatiable appetite for TV, DVDs, and violent video games.

The first family I worked with on *Shalom in the Home* were a good example of this phenomenon. They were a young Christian family with two highly involved parents and four seemingly well-behaved kids. Why, I wondered initially, had they even volunteered for the show? But the mother told me this story: They had gone to Cape Cod for a vacation, as they do every year. And midway through, she turned to her husband and asked him if he was having a good time. He said, "No, I'm not, and this is the last year we do any vacation at all. Between the constant fighting and the yelling to get them to listen, I feel more stressed out than I did before we left. I'd rather stay home than blow money this way."

These people seemed to have everything they could possibly want: a comfortable lifestyle, a nice house in a suburban neighborhood, healthy kids. The only thing missing was the greatest blessing of all, the blessing of peace. Without it, their home was a war zone. The parents I meet today are caught in the cross fire, and have lost all joy in parenting as a result.

Too few of us, it seems, are enjoying this thing we call family life. We are desperately in need of a new approach to parenting that is uniquely suited to these challenging times.

All is not lost, by any stretch of the imagination. There are many good parents out there, truly seeking answers. And their children want to be reached. So there is tremendous potential for both parties to heal and come together in a greatly repaired relationship, one that will make both of them—and the family unit as a whole—stronger. In this book, I am proposing the first steps toward a solution.

A MORE NATURAL STATE OF CHILDHOOD

Healing the American family will begin by restoring our children to a more natural, authentic state of childhood. As Hodding Carter so wisely wrote, we must give them both roots and wings. We must implement a parenting system that nourishes and protects them at the most fundamental levels, and then we must tap into our own passions and deeply held beliefs to inspire them to reach the greatest heights of their potential.

We must return our children to childhood by giving them a solid foundation of love and discipline coupled with the inspiration to grow.

Parenting isn't about molding lumps of formless clay into something virtuous and beautiful. Your child arrived in the world a complete original. She already inhabits Paradise, which I believe is not just a place but a metaphor for the innocence and perfection of childhood. Your job as a parent isn't to chip away at the marble of your child's personality until you unearth the beautiful sculpture within, but to facilitate the gradual unfolding of her potential by removing obstacles to her development and giving her all the support she needs.

If we don't raise our children, they have to raise themselves. And if we don't protect them from negative influences, they will be corrupted by those influences.

If we don't act as parents, then our children can't be kids.

I'm not talking (or not exclusively, anyway) about the physical protection of our children, but about protecting them morally and emotionally as well. Protection is the first branch of the PLANT method of parenting, the system I have developed to help us create stronger, more centralized families featuring happier, more relaxed parents, and children who finally have the freedom to be kids. As you will discover in this book, PLANT consists of five elements: Protection, Love, Activity, Novelty, and Tradition. These five ingredients, missing or sidelined in American family life today, are as essential to our children's well-being as food, water, and shelter.

Protection is not just the first branch of the PLANT parenting system, but the driving force behind the other four elements as well. We protect our children from insecurity by giving them the benediction of our unconditional Love. We protect them from boredom and listlessness by coming up with wholesome Activities—and by participating in those activities with them. We protect them from the relentless materialism and insatiability that destroys so many American lives and marriages by helping them to hold on to their innate sense of wonder, so that they can see Novelty by delving deeper into what they already have. And we protect them from loneliness and a feeling of purposelessness by giving them a sense of Tradition.

THE SPARK OF INSPIRATION

PLANT is the system that roots our kids into the ground, giving them a sense of unshakable security and a rock-solid foundation. But these five concepts, as important as they may be, are not the only ingredients necessary. Rather, it is the inspiration that we bring to our parenting that enables our children to soar like cedars and rise like redwoods.

Your job as a parent isn't just to pay for piano lessons, or to drive your son to soccer practice—it's to enable him to explore the full potential of his own personality and intelligence and capacity for love. Parenting doesn't just mean wiping your kid's nose and making sure that her socks match; it means throwing kindling on the spark of her potential and ardently fanning the ensuing blaze.

We must not simply police our children, we must inspire them.

If we simply superimpose our will on our children, they will feel coerced. If we forbid activities without supplying engaging substitutes, they will seek to escape us. If we bully our children into doing well, instead of bringing out a desire to contribute their unique gifts to the world, they will resent us. We must instead use inspiration so that they become willing participants—enthusiastic ones, even—in their own improvement.

Before Martin Luther King, Jr., it was customary in the black community to blame whites for the deplorable state of black life in the United States. And it was true, especially in the South, where bias and violence were so deeply entrenched in the social fabric that it seemed it would never change. But Dr. King's approach was different. He acknowledged the indisputable fact of white racism, but he did something else: he inspired the black community to lift themselves up. King understood that the black community lacked not only equal opportunity, but inspiration—and he knew that, given the right inspiration, they would demand and receive their legitimate rights as citizens of this country. And so he lit the world afire with the flame of his oratory, coaxing people out of their lethargy to march, and his passions, once transmitted, coalesced millions of people into a powerful movement. His greatness was in the inspiration that he provided—inspiration that ultimately changed the world.

Every parent is capable of inspiring their children, and we must now find this talent within ourselves and bring it to the forefront. We must instill in our children the desire to live a noble and meaningful life, and to live that life at the crest of the wave. Our conversations with our children must stir in them a love of justice and righteousness. Our dinner parties must motivate within our children a love for all of G-d's children. And our own behavior must model for them generosity, gratitude, and holiness—in short, the best possible version of adulthood.

Only then will they stop listlessly pushing green beans around their plates and participate in a vibrant, passionate dinner conversation. Only then will they be content to share their lives with their parents, and their parents' lives, instead of fleeing the family to gossip with their friends. Only then will our homes cease to be a collection of lonely individuals and become truly integrated into a *family*, whose bond is love and inspiration rather than blood and bones.

THE PROBLEM—AND THE SOLUTION

I understand that many of you may feel flummoxed or overwhelmed by the idea of this new responsibility. "My job bores me; I love my wife, but she bores me too. The state of the world depresses me. How in G-d's name am I supposed to inspire my kids?" Too many of us feel broken, mangled on the inside by a culture that values not our humanity but our money, not our hearts but our wallets, not our character but our productivity. When this is the version of adulthood that we present to our children, and the method by which we parent them, is it any surprise that we're raising kids who are listless, lethargic, and without hope for the future? Is there any wonder our kids look outside the home—to their friends and coaches at their school, or to the musicians and actors that paper their walls—for the inspiration they crave, for the passion they need, and for the motivation that is so sorely lacking at home?

But I believe that within the problem lies the kernel of a solution.

The road back to inspirational parenting—and indeed, an inspired life—is to spend more time with your kids.

Your children contain all the childlike qualities that the adult world has drummed out of you. They have unself-consciousness, optimism, and spontaneity to spare. They have endless enthusiasm and abundant energy. They have unfettered access to their emotions, and are as quick to giggle as they are to weep. And as Pablo Picasso said, all children are artists; they overflow with creativity and imagination. These qualities, which come so naturally to children, are what make them special, which is why it is so essential for us to protect and preserve these qualities in them.

But these qualities reside in us as well, and they're the flickers of the inspiration we need to be the parents our children need—and the people we ourselves need to be. All those attributes are still there, deep within us; they're just dormant, like the potential for heat within a lump of coal.

And the tinder we need to reanimate those magical qualities is right in front of us. It is our children's curiosity that will spark the interest and passion in life that we feel we've lost. It is our children's laughter that will fan the flames of our own joy, melting the icicles that have hardened around our hearts. And watching our children grow through innocent play will help us to rediscover, for all our obligations and responsibility, how we too are free.

In keeping our children safe from adulthood, we can ourselves find our way back to a more childlike state. And in warming ourselves by our children's glow, we will learn, once again, how to parent with fire.

CHILDHOOD REGAINED

CHAPTER ONE

*Finding Our Way Back
to the Garden of Eden*

> If we had paid no more attention to our
> plants than we have to our children, we
> would now be living in a jungle of weed.
> —Luther Burbank

Adults and children in America today feel they are staring at each other across a great divide. The sense of discomfort they feel around each other is palpable even to an outsider. They don't know what's going on in each other's lives. The relationship is adversarial instead of intimate, so that the very term "family" is beginning to lose any meaning.

Both adults and children in America today have lost touch with the magical qualities associated with childhood.

I consider it to be the central task of inspirational parenting to bring those qualities back to the forefront of our consciousness. Children need parents so that they can be children.

And parents, as I have said many times before, need children even more than they themselves are needed. We need our children to put us in contact with our fun-loving, innocent side—all the qualities that are extinguished by the difficulties and responsibilities of the adult world.

EARLY-ONSET ADULTHOOD

First, let us talk about the children. There is a crisis in American youth today.

The numbers of children involved in violent crime, drug abuse and treatment, and teen suicides indicate that our children are in a terrible amount of pain. According to the Centers for Disease Control and Prevention, 2.5 million children in America take drugs for ADHD—as many as take drugs for asthma.

It's gotten so bad that the most staggering statistics no longer even raise eyebrows. A few weeks after an eighth-grader in Pennsylvania walked into her school cafeteria with one of her father's guns and shot a classmate in the shoulder, I heard this statistic on NBC News: one in five teenage boys claimed not only to have easy access to a weapon, but to have taken one to school in the past year. And this didn't even make the top of the news; it was toward the end, near the human-interest story about the rescued kittens. Education, apparently, is no longer sacrosanct in this country, but just another way to jeopardize your life.

Even if the problems in your home are not so dramatic (as I hope they are not), can you honestly say that your kids are happy? Are they innocent and exuberant, the way children should be? Or do they seem bored and uninspired, lacking in creativity? Do they enjoy spending time with you and their siblings? Or do they flee the home to the tribe of friends that substitute for you?

You're not alone, and the problem is one that I call early-onset adulthood.

Our children are unhappy because they're not really kids at all, but cynical adults in disguise.

And that seems to be fine with them! Our children are blind to the pleasures of innocence and childhood, rushing instead to trade those things for the enticements of being grown-ups. Rather than being afraid that they'll miss out on their childhood years and the magic associated with them, our children seem to fear missing out *because* of their childhood years.

When you look at the culture around us, is it any surprise that this is happening? There are video games where you can loot, do drugs, rape prostitutes, and shoot policemen; a Top 40 dominated by sexualized children selling inappropriate records to other children; pornography on the billboards that line our streets; foul language and lascivious situations on broadcast television—and parents so overwhelmed or out to lunch that they don't raise a hand against this onslaught.

Well, children have always played at being grown-ups, you may say. But those aren't chocolate cigarettes they're smoking. We are seeing a real perversion in the natural progression of childhood, so that the children who, a mere year or two ago, were rocking and changing their Betsy Wetsy dolls are instead rocking and changing the real thing. And as our children assume adult roles, with none of the maturity that comes with adulthood, they're paying adult prices—in teen pregnancy, overdoses, and suicide.

I'm not willing to lie down and let the culture vultures have their way with my children. It's not the rapper's fault that our sons don't respect women, and it is not the teen idol's fault that our young daughters bare their midriffs and wear thong underwear. *We* must hold ourselves accountable for the current state of affairs, and *we* must take responsibility for what our children see and say and do. We may have, in the past, failed to inspire them to something better, but that's over now. Every one of us must—at long last—put our foot down and say, "No more. Not on my watch." It's time to bring the inspiration back to parenting, and childhood back to our children.

CHILDHOOD: A PARADISE LOST

Theologians and archaeologists have spent a great deal of time and effort searching for the physical location of the biblical Garden of Eden. What they have overlooked is that Paradise is right in front of us, and can be reclaimed at will. For the Garden of Eden is not only a place in space but a place in time. In short, it is our childhood.

Think, for a moment, about Adam and Eve. These first people were perfect, and perfectly innocent, without cynicism or embarrassment. They were utterly unself-conscious. They had no history, no lifetime of disappointments, no bitter resentments to get over. They knew no death or disease. They had everything they needed, including harmony with the beasts of the earth and the plants of the field.

They sound like children, don't they?

And so, another reading of the Garden of Eden is that it isn't a physical site, but a description of the Paradise that is childhood—a perception rather than a place, a moment in time rather than a location with a longitude and a latitude.

Paradise is a disposition, rather than a district.

When our kids can be fully children, they live in this Paradise. They aren't self-conscious, always worrying what others will think. They aren't judgmental, but view everyone on their own merits. They don't dissemble, or pretend they're not feeling what they're feeling. Instead, they have easy access to both joy and sadness. They are endlessly curious, filled with wonder and awe at the small miracles that fill our everyday lives—a fallen leaf, the explosion of a cherry tomato in their mouths, the white wonderland of an overnight snowfall. They have boundless energy for exploration and run for the sheer love of movement. They say what they mean and they mean what they say, and their only job is to laugh and be playful.

And that is the way it should be. But the children of America today, like Adam and Eve, have been expelled from the Garden of Eden. They have lost Paradise and entered the fallen world of adulthood. They have discovered embarrassment and emotional discomfort. They are no longer authentic. And they are no longer strangers to depression and disappointment.

THE CURSE OF INSATIABILITY

What was the act that led to Adam and Eve's expulsion from this place of innocence and perfection? Tempted by the snake, a symbol of adult greed and insatiability, *they acquired the wrong kind of knowledge,* just as our unsupervised children watch Paris Hilton's dirty home videos, listen to misogynist lyrics, watch a movie in which a cyborg uses human beings as shields. And it is through this knowledge that the hatred and corruption of the world makes itself known to our children, poisoning and corrupting them before their time.

As the medieval Jewish philosopher Maimonides pointed out, by deciding to eat the apple, Adam and Eve signaled that they had lost the ability to judge an objective truth. Morality became relative—"Although G-d said not to, eating this fruit might be okay under certain circumstances." Or, in more modern parlance, "It's okay to fool around with this boy because he says he really likes me," or "It's not like marijuana is heroin; nobody ever died from smoking a joint." With this illicit knowledge, Adam and Eve grew up, just as our children will. They closed the door to the idea of objective truth, to the difference between good and evil—and opened the door to subjective ones, which leads to such banner values as vanity, racism, and superficiality.

But perhaps most important, Adam and Eve lost the feeling of contentment and satisfaction that had sustained them—and it is here that I see a real echo in the problems facing our children today.

When G-d placed Adam and Eve in the Garden of Eden, He told them that they were allowed to eat from all of the trees—except one. For a while, they enjoyed their bounty. But along came the serpent, who said to them, in effect, "How can you guys be happy when there is still something you can't eat? Don't you feel deprived?" And so they focused on what they didn't have instead of what they did.

This was the beginning of their corruption, and their curse: to forever base their happiness not on internal joy but on external possessions. It is the curse of adulthood today as well. Kids are easily pleased—sure, they spend a lot of time crying for stuff they can't have, but by and large, they can be satisfied with something as simple as a story read aloud, or a boost up to the monkey bars at the park. What they really want is love and attention.

Adults, however, are insatiable. Their happiness is dependent on how much money they get, how many things they can buy with that money, or how many people they can sleep with. Even the moguls of this world, with all their power and money, can find no happiness because they are never content. The wives they marry are never young or pretty enough, the bank accounts they have are never large enough, their children are never good enough, which is why so many successful parents ruin their kids.

In the Bible, when G-d punishes the serpent, He curses him to slither on his belly for all eternity. The insatiable man or woman does not walk; they are no longer independent and erect, because their happiness is entirely dependent on what they acquire today, even as they grow completely bored of it tomorrow. Without anything sturdy and of real value to prop them up, they fall to their bellies, and in that state they crawl through their miserable lives, believing they have made progress. The man on television may appear to be a high-and-mighty billionaire, but if you look closely, you can see him slithering. He spends his entire time bragging about how much money he has. He dates and marries trophy women. He puts his name on everything. Really, what he is saying is, "I acknowledge that I have no inner dignity. So I am doing my best to get your attention with what I have on the outside."

The serpent is also cursed to eat dust. On the one hand, it would seem that he has an abundance of sustenance, since dust is so plentiful, just as the billionaire is surrounded by money, so much that it can never run out. But the money, just like dust, is deeply unsatisfying. You make and make it, buy big houses and private jets with it, and still you feel empty inside. So the serpent is cursed with eating something that is ultimately not fulfilling. He is condemned to insatiability just as all those who are bitter with his toxic poison are similarly cursed.

When we starve our children of the love they need and deserve, they become just like that billionaire, substituting mere stuff for parental affection. And we only exacerbate this when we play the role of the serpent: "If you make the team, I'll get you that new Xbox." "If you do well at school, I'll take you to Disney World." What's on offer is always something unimportant that the child does not have, rather than the love and affection that the child really needs. And so the child—*while still a child*—turns into a miniature version of the insatiable adults who surround him.

The biggest difference that I can see between Adam and Eve and our children is that Adam and Eve instantly perceived what they had lost, and begged G-d for a second chance. Our children, by contrast, beg us for looser restrictions. They think they are empowering themselves by taking on this inappropriate knowledge, but of course the precise opposite is really true.

There is nothing so powerful as an unsullied childhood and all that it confers: a sturdy foundation, the freedom to explore without fear, and faith in the future. And it can last forever, long after our children have grown into their adult bodies. Because the greatest gift of a real childhood is the ability to internalize this critical phase of life and carry it into the future.

Aren't some of the most successful men and women those who have stayed in touch with their inner child? I think, for instance, of Steven Spielberg and George Lucas, filmmakers who know how to communicate with children because they have never lost their childish access to emotions, imagination, and sense of play. I think too of two of the most brilliant scientific minds of the last century: Albert Einstein, with his tousled hair and his utter disregard for adult conventions, and Richard Feynman, the celebrated American physicist, an irrepressible practical joker whose groundbreaking research was inspired by the wobble of a Frisbee. Michelangelo, Picasso, Mozart, Brahms, Beethoven—all of these men were famous for their childlike natures. They were playful, curious, imaginative, creative, and endlessly energetic—kids in adult bodies.

Every one of us starts our life in the state of mind that is Paradise. And every one of us is eventually expelled, as we grow older and join the cynical, often corrupt world of adults. But when we have a real childhood, we never really leave childhood behind.

And our fall from grace does not need to happen so soon.

19

I see my primary parental role as the protector of my children. Yes, I am there to love and support them, to entertain and educate them—but my primary role is to make sure they are safe, physically, emotionally, and spiritually. For me, that means extending their stay in Paradise for as long as I possibly can. I will not permit the insidious influence of the serpent into my house; I will throw my own body on the apple as if it were a grenade.

We will talk, in the Protection section of the PLANT (the ancient rabbis actually say the fruit was a fig) parenting method, of ways to protect our children. But my real goal, through inspirational parenting, is to open my children's eyes to the Paradise that already surrounds them, so that they don't trade their true freedom for the false liberties of adulthood.

Let the archaeologists search. I know that the Garden of Eden exists, to this very day, here on earth. I see it in my son Yosef's eyes, I hear it in my daughter Rochel Leah's laughter, I witness it in my daughter Shaina's curiosity and know that it can be regained whenever a teenager's bravado and posturing falls away and a child stands before me.

THE BROKEN AMERICAN PARENT

It is our job as parents to inspire our children to explore the joys of childhood instead of prematurely trading it in for the soiled trials of adulthood. I know it's not easy. Too often, we adults find that we are ourselves without inspiration. This, I believe, is because we have lost touch with our own inner child.

Some of us are able to keep a small piece of Paradise at our core, retaining a child's sense of awe and wonder, even as we grow into the responsibilities of adulthood. But most of us are not so lucky: what remains of our inner child shrinks down to a hard, shriveled kernel, found somewhere to the east of our spleen. In fact, when you look at modern American adulthood, it's surprising that our children are throwing themselves headlong into it—one glimpse of what awaits them should be enough to send them hightailing it back to the womb.

We live in a culture of competition. Our status is determined by externals: how much our house cost, how new our car is, how big our corner office is. In order to lay our hands on these externals, we must make some terrible trade-offs, sacrificing our dignity and all the things that really matter for money and recognition. After all, helping your kids with their homework won't help you claw your way to the top.

If you don't secure those externals—either because you're dedicated to staying a decent person or simply because you're unsuccessful professionally, you're left to feel worthless. The culture rewards money, power, and prestige, not the honest businessman, the devoted husband, the involved father. So you escape, becoming a sports fanatic or a workaholic, convincing yourself that you're living vicariously through your team, or that one more hour in the office will give you the success you crave.

Or you look outside of your family for satisfaction. Maybe the attentions of another woman will make you feel like a winner. Your wife can't do that for you; after all, she married *you*, not someone really important. So she must be as big a loser as you are, right? And she's too exhausted for affection and sex, anyway. Like you, she works hard to bring home a second income, and then arrives home to her "other job," keeping the house afloat. Overwhelmed by her responsibilities, she either turns into a shouter, browbeating you and your kids to help with chores, or a martyr, who suffers in guilt-inducing, passive-aggressive silence.

Something has to give, and it is usually her sense of self, as she slowly loses her individuality and morphs into a chauffeur, chef, and sheriff—all stuff that she resents you for, and that you can use against her later, when you explain why you're leaving her for someone younger and trimmer. Small wonder that, according to the *Washington Post*, one in three doctor-office visits by women involves a prescription for an antidepressant!

The American marriage is in trouble, and that trouble trickles down immediately to our kids. Bereft as both of you are of inspiration, you fail to inspire your children. Instead, you act like cops, admonishing them for everything they do wrong or fail to do right. So they spend more and more time with their friends, away from the family, and look elsewhere for heroes: sports figures, actors, and musicians.

For me, the great tragedy of this scenario is how unnecessary it all is. Because you are both heroes; you just don't know it. You—not the guy with the twenty-two-inch vertical leap, or the billionaire who divorces his third wife weeks before her settlement will increase, or the actor who commands millions of dollars per film—should have the book deals and the wall posters and the world tours. But you don't, and you've swallowed the poisonous lie that your good deeds don't matter because they won't end up in a newspaper.

This crisis is destroying America's families.

All around me, I see a generation of broken men, married to lonely women, raising insecure children.

And the cycle is intensifying, so that every generation becomes more and more dependent on externals to make them feel valuable.

But I believe that broken things can be fixed, and I have the utmost faith that the American family can be mended. That healing will begin with the understanding that success in life is measured not by the quantity of our bank accounts but the quality of our relationships, and the understanding that to be human is not to acquire but to connect.

Who knows this better than a child? A child's allegiance is to the person who loves and cherishes her, regardless of how much that person's shoes cost. A child looks for someone who can bring a storybook to life, not someone with a million dollars in the bank. These are the qualities that inspirational parenting will help you to safeguard in your children. And by making sure that we preserve them in our children, we ensure that they're not absent from our lives either.

THE WAY BACK

We're no fools. We know that something precious is missing. In fact, most of us are engaged in a desperate search for what we have lost. But we're looking in all the wrong places. We can't get back to Paradise by injecting poison into our foreheads; Botox can never erase the experiences that gave us those lines. We can play adult versions of the games we played as children, but we can't parasail or bungee jump our way back to the Garden of Eden. We will never get the pleasure from our Mercedes Maybachs that we got from our Matchbox cars, and the eternal bachelor who plays video games and eats potato chips for dinner won't rediscover his childhood by eluding adult responsibility.

Of course we can't find our way back to Paradise with solutions that lack substance. But we need look no further, because the answer is right in front of us: our children. We simply have to change our perspective, so that we recognize that our children are the antidote for a great deal of the poison in our lives.

Our children can show us the road back to Paradise.

The Bible says that after G-d expelled Adam and Eve from the Garden of Eden, He placed the cherubim—angels with baby faces—at the gates of Paradise to protect it. Those cherubim are our children; they are the GPS navigation way back to Paradise. They can help us to access the kernel of hope and innocence that is left over from our childhoods; they can help us to feed and water that seed so that it sprouts, grows, and flourishes.

Even the simplest gesture can serve to germinate that seed. I recently went through a particularly acrimonious contract negotiation. People I had worked with before, whom I liked and thought I could trust, were behaving in shockingly hurtful ways, and after a few days of back-and-forth, I felt brutalized: old, cynical, and depressed.

I went downstairs to get a cup of coffee—but as soon as I appeared in the kitchen, I found myself underneath a pile of children who were hell-bent on incorporating me into their game, the goal of which seemed to be making a rude noise on someone else's stomach. I was, of course, the ultimate prize, and no match for them working as a team. For the first time in days, I felt the cares of the adult world lift from my shoulders, and I laughed—really laughed.

What a gift! Medical experts say that children laugh about four hundred times a day; adults, by contrast, average about fifteen. On that particular day, I doubt I had even cracked a smile. But the sheer giddiness and joy of being a child transmitted itself from my children to the kernel of Paradise held over from my own childhood. So infected, I went back to my negotiations with a lighter heart.

And what better solution is there to our constant feelings of inadequacy and meaninglessness than to bring a child into the world and raising him or her to become a functioning member of your family and the society at large? Our children give us a sense of purpose like nothing else on earth. I know of course that parents often get tired, and are often frustrated by their children. I know how crushing the weight of responsibility can sometimes feel, but I have noticed something interesting: I very rarely hear parents question whether their lives have meaning.

Of course parents don't have to ask questions of the "Why do I exist?" variety; the answer is sitting next to them, eating cornflakes. But I can't count the number of Wall Street big hitters who have sailed into their forties on a wave of champagne and strip clubs, and now come to me desperate—"Shmuley, will you help me to find someone to share my life with?" Their bonuses and 401(k)s may not steal the sports section and conceal how badly they're doing in algebra, but they don't give big good-night hugs either.

Our children need us to guide them, so that they can hold on to the Paradise that is childhood for as long as they possibly can. Safeguarding their childhoods allows them to keep a child at their center, even as they grow up. Like all adults, they will inevitably suffer disappointment and heartache. They too will have to pay taxes and suffer the indignities of the aging body. Indeed, it is one of the hardest lessons of parenting that we cannot protect our children from the setbacks and losses they will inevitably suffer. But if we defend their childhoods so that they can take a little bit with them always, then we give them something very rich indeed—a memory of Paradise that they can seek to re-create, no matter how old they are. And we need them to reintroduce us to that glory, so that we can escape the crushing demands and ugliness of the adult world.

In the chapters that follow, I will introduce you to the PLANT parenting method. Each letter stands for one of the five branches of the method: Protection, Love, Activity, Novelty, and Tradition.

Unlike some other methods, PLANT focuses on building healthier families, not just better kids. And while that may require more of you than some other parenting methods, it will also bring greater rewards, because PLANT is not just a way to help our children hold on to the childhood that is rightfully theirs, but a way for us as parents to regain the best aspects of what we have lost.

What I am calling for is for parents and children to meet halfway, and I believe that the tenets of inspirational parenting can help us to find that glorious middle ground. For some, the middle is a form of compromise, but for me, it is a form of synthesis. For parents and children to meet in the middle is to bring together the best of both worlds: adult drive and childlike playfulness; adult vision and child-like innocence; adult responsibility and childlike creativity; adult experience and childlike optimism. And it is of such meetings that fiery families are made.

PROTECTION

CHAPTER TWO

Making a World That Is Safe for a Child

Once you bring life into the world, you must protect it.
We must protect it by changing the world.
—Elie Wiesel

Many parents mistakenly believe that the first job of a parent is to love their children.

They're wrong.

In this book, I will call for a radical redefinition of our responsibility toward our children, and that redefinition begins right here: **Our primary job as parents is not to love our children, but to *protect* them.**

Don't misunderstand me: the unconditional love we give our children is essential and without substitute; our children have a fundamental need to know they are loved, completely and without reservation. Most important, they need to know that we extend that love not because of what they do or how they do it, but simply because they *are*. Loving our children in this way instills a sense of security that cannot be shaken, and gives them a true measure of their own value, so that they never have to believe that money or accomplishments are the currencies by which they may purchase self-esteem.

But unconditional love is just one side of the coin. We dare not forget that the sapling, small and fragile, needs to be protected from the fierce winds. All the watering in the world won't rescue a plant that has been uprooted; there's nothing to love if the object of your love is destroyed. So contrary to what you may now believe, the very first job of a parent is not to love your child, but to *protect* your child from harm. Your role as guardian comes before any other.

The urge to protect our children is as natural and intuitive as the overpowering sense of love we feel toward them. Yes, when your infant was placed into your arms for the first time, your heart moved in love. But everyone I've ever spoken to also experienced another overwhelming sensation—the knowledge that you, and you alone, were responsible for the care and well-being of this astonishingly vulnerable and fragile being. As you looked down into that tiny, wrinkled face, you understood that you had been charged with the most solemn duty of all, to protect and nurture this child to adulthood, to the very best of your ability.

Protecting our children is a duty we cannot shirk. But what does it really mean? For me, it means creating a world that is safe for your child.

It is our first responsibility as adults to create a world that is safe for children.

Now, we have a fairly clear understanding of what that means when we're talking about younger children. We take basic precautionary measures, as a matter of course, gating the stairs, blocking electrical outlets, and shutting away poisonous cleaning supplies. We drop our kids off at school and wait till they're safely inside; we teach them to look both ways before they cross the street.

I met with a young mother a few weeks ago. As soon as she arrived, she set down a clean quilt on the living room carpet, along with appropriately chewable playthings, and while we talked, her young son got to work banging and gumming and shaking the toys, conducting all the baby experiments so important to his development. By creating a clean, safe, well-padded environment for her son to explore under her watchful guidance, she had created a world that was safe for her child.

There was nothing extraordinary about what she did—except it highlighted for me how delinquent so many of us are in our duties to our children as they get older. Where is the soft quilt where our children can safely explore the world as they move into puberty? Where is the environment that will allow our teens to feel as secure and as supervised as our infants? Of course parenting would be much easier if our teenagers stayed where we put them and were contented as long as they had a variety of brightly colored, chewable objects to play with! But are we really doing all we can to provide them with the equivalent: a clean, well-supervised place, where it is safe for them to be children?

I think not. Although we seem to be paying a lot of attention to protecting our children, we're actually closing the barn door long after the horse has escaped. By putting a disproportionate amount of our energy into worrying about physical threats, we actually expose our children to a series of much greater risks.

THE WAGES OF FEAR

The first risk is to our relationships. The fearmongering so favored by our politicians and the news media causes incredible stress between parents and children. To parent in the early part of the twenty-first century is to see a sexual predator around every corner, deathly microbes in every salad bar, and bird flu in every childhood cough. It's terrifying! And if it's not, we're made to feel that we're doing something wrong by not being vigilant enough.

Please, don't get me wrong: protecting our children from physical harm is an important part of the job description. Tragically, there are parents who, through neglect or actual abuse, fail to uphold their end of this unwritten covenant, and I can think of nothing that is sadder, or more a violation of the natural order of things. But my comments here are not for those parents; it is for those of us who are trying to negotiate the balance between taking legitimate precautions to safeguard our children and succumbing to a host of irrational fears.

When I talk to parents these days, it seems like the primary emotion they feel toward their kids is anxiety. They're worried that something bad is going to happen to them. They worry that they won't get into good colleges. If their kids are difficult, they worry they'll alienate them by setting boundaries and enforcing rules. And when there's nothing to worry about, they worry about why their kids aren't rebelling. Some of these concerns are valid, some aren't, but many of the parents I meet seem to believe that worrying about these things casts some kind of protective spell on their children.

But perhaps we should be protecting our children from our concern. Because when the primary emotion you feel around your kids is anxiety, it's impossible to have fun with them, and that's a sorry state of affairs—for both parties. In fact, I think this culture of fear is one of the reasons parents aren't enjoying their roles more. I *love* hanging out with my kids. It's the most fun I have. It's fun to take them swimming or out for an informal dinner. But if I allow my worries about sharks and E. coli to take over, spending time with them quickly becomes a worrisome chore—and that's no good, for my kids or for me.

When we're such nervous Nellies, is it any surprise that our kids don't want to hang out with us? Would you choose to be with someone who spent most of their time with you listing all the ways you could come to an untimely end?

If being with you isn't an activity that your children enjoy, for the most part, you not only lose the opportunity to influence them and impart your values, but you lose the opportunity to learn from and enjoy your children, one of the greatest gifts I know. I believe that we have to change our parenting styles, not just to give our kids the best chance, but so that we can take more enjoyment from them ourselves. Our kids shouldn't be the only winners, and when you parent inspirationally, they're not. So break your six o'clock news habit; those alarmist bulletins that weigh so heavily on your mind aren't helping you or your kids. Your kids are safest when they're spending time with you, playing with you, interacting with you, and learning from you—not when you're worrying about them. And enjoying them is the way to a happier relationship with them as well.

But there is a larger, more important risk looming than the harm fear does to our relationship with our children. We can no longer allow our focus on their physical safety—as important as that safety is—to distract us from the equally serious dangers they face elsewhere. We have allowed ourselves to become blinded by the culture of fear and by what we perceive as physical dangers—to the point of obsession. But we have failed to notice or prevent a number of very real dangers, dangers that have already invaded the shelter of our homes, and that immediately threaten the safety of our children.

It's ten o'clock: do you know what your kids are watching?

I think that even rational, sensible people find that they are susceptible to fearmongering because it echoes the quiet voice, buried somewhere deep inside all of us, that is telling us we're not really doing the best job we can to create a world that is truly safe for our children.

Tell me: what is the point of protecting your children from external dangers when they are exposed, each and every day, to influences that will destroy them from the inside? Look around, and you will find that modern parenting is rife with paradoxes. You triple-check the babysitter's references and credit history, but let your kid disappear for hours with her friends at the mall. You buy only organic milk and vegetables, but have no idea what kind of misogynistic trash is playing on your tween's iPod. You drop your kids off at school so the bogeyman doesn't get them—and then take them to an R-rated movie, where they can see him do drugs and have sex.

We say that we would do anything to ensure our children's safety, and yet we stand idly by while a sewer of grime and muck is pumped directly into their vulnerable cerebral cortexes, courtesy of the Internet, the PS2, and our friendly neighborhood cineplex.

Sometimes it seems to me as if the world has turned upside down. Certainly, parents today seem to have become inured to the corrosive influences surrounding their kids. I have met parents who allow their kids to be sexually active in their very early teens, permitting sleepovers with boyfriends and even helping them to secure birth control. I've seen parents spoil their kids rotten by giving them thousands of dollars' worth of stuff—without ever once asking them to do something to earn it. I have met parents who smoke marijuana with their teenagers.

How long can we pretend that we're not colluding in the theft of our children's most valuable attribute: their innocence?

Here's a reality check for you: it is *not* normal for your kids to be having more sex than you are. Parenting is *not* supposed to be something farmed out to the purposeless proxies of television, movies, and video games. We all want to be able to afford material comforts, but giving your kids "the things you never had" should mean a good education, direction, and inspiration, *not* a platinum card without a spending limit.

When we treat our children as if they were young

adults—a term that should be used sparingly—rather than as kids, we are allowing them to skip their childhoods, a stage that is absolutely essential to giving them a strong foundation for adulthood. If we want well-mannered, intellectually curious, and spiritually secure children that we can take real pride in, we will have to take action now, working toward a world that is *truly* safe. That safety may start with window guards and a locked medicine cabinet, but it cannot end there.

Exposure to gratuitous violence, sex, and other uniquely adult subjects overwhelms children with emotions and experiences they cannot digest, sowing confusion and anxiety. It also imparts to them an inauthentic desire to prematurely discard the wonders of their youth and join an adult world that is all about compromises.

We have to shield our children from the increasingly malign influences of a culture that is telling them, subtly but constantly, to skip childhood. It is up to us to slow down their rush to grow up by safeguarding their innocence. We do this by committing to raising our children rather than forcing them to raise themselves. We have to reembrace our role as protector and guardian, placing it before every other parental role.

Your ten-year-old kid wants to watch an R-rated movie. You know it's wrong; he's too young. But you see how badly he wants it, and you dread what will happen if you say no. So you give in, and he ends up absorbing images that he is simply not old enough to assimilate. You've avoided a fight—a good example of winning the battle but losing the war.

Your fourteen-year-old daughter wants to go away for the weekend with her boyfriend's family. You know it's a stupid idea. The boyfriend's parents are much more lax than you are in chaperoning them, and there will be no one to make sure your daughter isn't pressured into doing something she doesn't really want to do. You know the statistics that nearly 50 percent of all young teens in America have given and received oral sex. And you know that there is even a strong and serious linkage between teen sexual activity and suicide. But you cave in because you don't want to deprive your daughter, or because you can't bear to have the battle with her, and she ends up losing something irreplaceable: her innocence.

A woman who was a teen sex expert—can you believe there is such a thing?—came on my radio show to promote her new book on teen sexuality. She told me on the air that her fourteen-year-old daughter had come to her recently to say that she had decided to have full intercourse with her fifteen-year-old boyfriend, and wanted her mother to go with her to the doctor to get contraception. "What did you say to your daughter?" I asked the big expert. "I told her that I thought it was a bad idea for her to have sex so early, and that she should consider doing other things with him that didn't involve full penetration. But at the end of the day, it was her decision and that if she did want to have sex, I would help her learn all the facts so that she could avoid pregnancy and disease."

I could hardly believe what I was hearing. If I were writing the subtitles for that conversation, here's what they'd say: "Hi, Mom. I want to ruin my life by having sex way too early with a boy who is too young to even know how to love me." The mother's response: "Okay. Let me help you sign up for the Pill." This woman was not her daughter's friend, but her enemy.

Safe sex doesn't just mean avoiding death and pregnancy. It means making sure that your heart doesn't die. It means making sure that you're not used at fourteen by some pimply moron who wants to take masturbating to the next level. Safe sex means learning to respect yourself as a woman, and not giving in to the pressure of lecherous men. It means having boys your age respect you as a peer with a brain, not letting them treat you like an X-rated blow-up doll. As far as I'm concerned, this so-called expert had utterly forfeited her role as protector, and had allowed egregious harm to her vulnerable young daughter as a result. Modern parenting, she called it. I call it criminal negligence.

I don't allow my daughters to date. Period. For me, this rule isn't even about protecting them physically, it's about protecting them mentally and emotionally. I don't want them to have to be subject to the approval of the opposite sex before they've had the opportunity to make up their own minds about things, before their own identities have had the chance to gel and set. I don't want popularity among the opposite sex to have any bearing on their self-esteem before they have had a chance to discover their intrinsic selves. Sexuality is a powerful force, and there is plenty of time for it later, when they are married to men who love them. But while they are still children, I want them to enjoy the freedoms of childhood without the encumbrances of the adult world.

GIVING THEM WHAT THEY *REALLY* WANT

They may not look like it, but children of all ages are crying out to be taken care of. When we cave in and let them watch the inappropriate movie, play the violent video game, or sleep over at the boyfriend's house, we may think we're giving them what they really want, but indeed, the opposite is actually true. It may seem that they just want to be left alone, that they want unrestricted freedom and unbridled indulgence. That's what they tell us, and that's what we choose to believe. But deep inside, children want to be protected, because it is only when they have that protection that they can fully enjoy the defenselessness and vulnerability that are a child's prerogative.

In a world where there are no parents, there can be no children.

And we can see the consequences of our neglect for ourselves. Of course our kids are acting out—they're furious with us for failing to protect them!

I have noticed that bath time for a toddler is almost always bookended by a lot of naked chasing; no matter the temperature, kids love to feel their bodies without the armor of clothes and socks and shoes. To wallow in vulnerability like that is true freedom, a freedom that adults haven't known since the Garden of Eden. That lack of self-consciousness isn't reserved for very small children (although, thankfully, the nudity usually is); I revel in the openness my children show in the way they interact with the world. It's an openness that is only possible when they know they are secure in the safe space of childhood, with someone watching over them.

This freedom, unfortunately, is too easily lost. How many young girls refuse to do cannonballs and splash in the pool because they're embarrassed by how they look in a bathing suit? How many spend hours preparing for school by doing their hair and makeup, as if they were going to be judged on how sexy they look instead of the intelligence of the questions they ask? How many teens take up cigarettes, drugs, and sexual behavior simply because they want to look cool in a world where cool is equated with looking old before your time?

Your children want someone to stop them from harming themselves. They want the freedom to be children, and to have that freedom, they need someone to say no to all the unwholesome pursuits that would steal it from them. If not you, the parent, then who?

My television show has brought me in contact with some of the very dangerous ideas that have snuck into the common wisdom about parenting. One of the most pernicious is the idea that children should act as coparents, with equal say in the decisions made on their behalf.

With one family in New York, we found that the three-year-old was quite literally running the house. To give an example, he had no set bedtime, and would run around until eleven o'clock at night. When I asked his father why he didn't simply enforce an earlier bedtime, he acted like I was a heartless Neanderthal or some kind of fascist. "I want my son to participate in the decision about what time he should go to bed," he told me. "Bedtime should be negotiated, and mutually agreed upon."

My first reaction, truthfully, was to laugh. This three-year-old, apparently, was Henry Kissinger, and I was the idiot. Since when does a three-year-old know what's best for him? But when I saw more of this parenting theory in action, it seemed considerably less funny to me. Expecting their

three-year-old to "collaborate" on his own parenting was rip-
ping their family apart and dangerously confusing their son.

How did this happen? How did we come to believe that
we'd be acting against our children's best interests by making
and enforcing rules? When did we come to confuse over-
permissiveness with love? Why are we so afraid to act like
parents?

Please—don't think I don't know how difficult and how
unpleasant it can be to do the right thing. Learning to discipline my children has unquestionably been the hardest part
of being a parent. But I do make strict rules about what my
children can and cannot do and what will happen if those
rules are disobeyed, because I understand that this is what I
must do if I am to satisfy my primary responsibility as their
parent: to protect them from harm.

Many of us shirk our disciplinary responsibilities because
of one simple fact: it doesn't feel good. Most of us are blessed
with great compassion and sympathy toward our children,
and it feels like disciplining them is in violation of those feelings. I remember one night a long time ago, when my daughters Chana and Mushki were two and three years old,
respectively. I was the rabbi at Oxford University then, and
our house was always filled with students. The students loved
to play with our little girls, who would naturally always want
to be out where the action was. But they had begun to stay
up too late at night, so that they weren't getting enough
sleep, and we found ourselves with irritable, sleep-deprived
toddlers in the morning. So I had a conversation with my
wife about it, and we decided to enforce an earlier bedtime.

We were unsuccessful the first night. The girls let themselves out of their room after we had put them to bed and came to sit with the students in the living room. So the next night we set up a child safety gate, so that they wouldn't be able to escape their bedroom. And although it was fifteen years ago, I remember the scene that night as if it were yesterday—my beautiful little girls, crying and climbing on each other, trying to get out from behind the prison fence I myself had erected! I was heartbroken, and would probably have set them free, but my wife reminded me that we were acting in their best interests; we weren't doing them any favors by allowing them to stay up too late, so that they didn't have the energy or concentration to play and learn in the daytime. And of course it was the right thing to do, even if it did feel terrible at the time. So we came back to their bedroom time and again to put them into their beds and made it clear that if they got out again they would be punished. Once they understood that "no" meant "no," they put themselves to bed, and we had no more trouble (and no more cranky mornings) after that.

It's easy to roll over, to minimize the consequences that will follow if we acquiesce. But it's important for us to stay strong; we're the last line of defense! Of course your children will try to throw off the yoke of your protection—it's their job to seek independence and freedom. But we have to protect our children as passionately as we love them and play with them.

Discipline isn't something you enforce because you hate your kids—it's something you do *because you love them*.

That's what the father of that insomniac three-year-old needed to understand. He was a loving parent—and at some level, a good one—but he and his wife were parenting out of fear. They were afraid of being firm with their son because they thought it might mean losing him, or at least losing his affection. It later turned out that the father had had a bad relationship with his own father, and that his wife had been—literally—left on a bus as an infant. Talk about abandonment issues; no wonder these two loving parents were afraid to get tough with their son.

In my experience, enforcing rules is hardest when we feel that we're doing less than a perfect job of parenting to begin with. Let's say I have to spend a period of time away from my kids, as I sometimes do when I'm on a book tour or shooting the television show. They'll call me and ask to watch something special on television. Now, we have a hard-and-fast rule about no television during the week in our house, but when I'm away, I feel like I have to console them for my absence. I'm tempted to give in, but I recognize that I'm softening to make myself feel better—and why should they pay for my insecurities as a father? It may be harder for me to put my foot down when I am away, but I remind myself that it is especially important to hold the line when I can't be there to inspire in person.

The same thing is true about disciplining them when I get home from a trip. I've missed them—I don't want to spend the time we do have together punishing them for some infraction! But that's a very selfish way to think. My children don't exist on this planet to make me happy; they're not playthings. I have a responsibility to them that I have to execute, whether or not it interferes with the nicer plans I might have had for our evening together.

Many parents tell me they hesitate to enforce rules because they are afraid of opening themselves up to charges of hypocrisy. "I can't tell him not to smoke; it's hypocritical of me to expect him to do what I can't," one father told me. Another mother confessed that she felt like a phony warning her daughter about the dangers of alcohol and drugs because she'd spent her teenage years getting drunk and stoned with her friends.

But this is a very dangerous path to go down. We did a show that featured a man who felt he couldn't put his foot down with his daughter and her boyfriend—they were having sex already at sixteen—because he had destroyed their family by cheating on his wife. He felt he had lost his moral authority, and with it, any right to tell his daughter what she could and could not do with her body. I said to him what I say to the rest of these parents who allow their own actions and history to prevent them from acting as a parental authority: "The point is not to feel guilty about the bad things you've done in your life, but to *fix* them. You feel you cannot take your daughter in hand because of your previous actions—I say they give you the ultimate authority. Who knows better than you how damaging sex can be without love and respect? You have an opportunity to heal your child, and through her, to heal the world. Take it!" It was very moving to see him as he laid down the law with his daughter's boyfriend, ensuring that the boy would show her the respect she deserves and cease all pressure to have her cater to his physical needs—and in so doing, began to heal his own relationship with his daughter.

It is our job as parents to draw the line, and to do the best thing for our children—whether it makes us hypocrites or not, and whether they appreciate it or not. If your children break free and begin running toward the street, you don't feel badly about grabbing their arms roughly, hauling them back out of harm's way, and using your most stern voice to warn them about the dangers of oncoming cars, do you? Why then do you feel so guilty enforcing rules about what they can watch, when they can begin dating, or what they can wear out of the house? This, too, is protection of the highest order.

GETTING BACK TO THE GARDEN OF EDEN

Children in America are furious with their parents—but not because they didn't get the DVDs they wanted for Christmas, or because their curfew isn't late enough. They're furious because they know—innately—they've lost their childhood. They know instinctively that they've been robbed of something unique, special, and irreplaceable—kicked out of the Garden of Eden, long before their time.

Adam and Eve were not successful in making their way back to the Garden of Eden, but I believe there is a more hopeful future for our children. My solution is simple, and can be captured in a single sentence: *Get rid of the junk.* Get rid of the junk culture, the junk ideas, the junk expectations.

Impossible? It's not. Here are some of the things we do in our house.

Ban television during the week. My kids are allowed to watch "the boob tube" only as a special treat on weekends. Even then, it's programming I have approved of in advance, and my wife and I usually watch it with them.

Not everything that comes out of the entertainment industry is without merit; find something that reflects your own interests and values. Try to make it intelligent! I have been fairly unimpressed with what passes for children's entertainment—while these shows and movies may not have explicitly "adult themes," I'm not sure that I consider jokes about flatulence and animal poop to be any more elevating than jokes about sex and drugs.

If we watch movies, for instance, it's usually within a larger context. For instance, I took the family on a trip to Jamestown, Virginia, which was established in 1607 as one of the very first English colonies. So when the feature film *The New World*, a retelling of the story of the relationship between Pocahontas and the adventurer John Smith during the early days of Jamestown, was released, I took my kids to see it as a special treat. I was astonished to see how their knowledge of the real-life history behind the movie turned it from a disposable confection into a subject they could discuss at great length and with considerable heat.

I always laugh when I hear about new couples going on movie dates—what can you possibly learn about each other while you're sitting in the dark? I feel the same way about families, and caution parents to make sure that movies, television, and other media become a reason to talk to one another—not a way to avoid face-to-face conversation. You can do this by using whatever you watch as a launchpad for discussions. Go for dinner or ice cream afterward, and engage your children on what they've just seen. What did you think of the ending? What would you have done with the money? Do you think she should have chosen the quiet guy instead? Allow this time together to provide opportunities for the conversations you want to have with your kids about the big issues in life: love, morality, charity, the importance of meaningful work.

Keep trash magazines and trash culture out of your house. If you read tabloid crap about damaged celebrities, your kids will too. If you watch mind-numbing sitcoms, depraved dramas, or reality TV that shows the very worst face of humanity, your kids will take that as tacit permission to do so themselves. Your kids don't need it, and you don't either.

Spoil them, but in your own way. Our family spends a small fortune at Barnes and Noble; I often joke that our local store is going to change the name to *Boteach* and Noble. But for us, it's money well spent. First of all, going to the bookstore is a family outing, and a fun one. Choosing books is something everyone enjoys; we are united in a common activity, but can also pursue our own varied interests. And it doesn't stop there; we go home to spend time together as a family, lying on the couches and on blankets in the living room and reading the books we've brought home.

Another family I know puts the money that they'd spend on entertainments like movies and magazines toward a family skiing trip; the children are avid snowboarders. So a couple of times a year, they enjoy days filled with vigorous exercise, capped off by a family dinner and an early bedtime—much more wholesome than Saturdays spent blowing money at the mall! And the parents find it much more agreeable to splurge on a present like a new parka or á better board than belly shirts and DVDs.

Change your expectations. Will someone tell me where

it is written that a child will instantly turn into a demon when he hits puberty?

The "teenager," and now the "tween," are marketing concepts, not parenting ones.

Unlike many of my peers, I do not assume that my children will turn into screaming, door-slamming maniacs when they turn thirteen. I do not assume that my children will be embarrassed to be seen with me in public. I do not assume that my children will shrink from showing me physical affection in front of their friends. In short, I protect them—and myself—from the cultural expectations that would fracture our family, and I suggest that you do too.

The psychological need to separate from parents is a real thing—as are the hormones that accompany this phase of life. But in our house, you are always expected to behave like a citizen. You can be having a bad day, but that does not mean you are exempt from your responsibilities, like helping to clear the table or speaking kindly to your siblings. Period. End of story. And by the way, that includes the parents.

CAREFULLY SCRUTINIZE YOUR KIDS' FRIENDS

When a kid is "bad," are the parents to blame?

I think they are. "But, Shmuley," other parents tell me, "we can't control them the way we could when they were little. We're not their only influence once they go out into the world. They spend eight hours a day with their friends at school! How can we possibly counter whatever influence their friends have?"

Maybe you can't. But in that case, it seems crucially important that you know who those friends are. I like to invite my children's friends to Shabbos dinner so they can stay through the weekend. I like to talk to them, get to know them, and find out what they're interested in. I also like to see what the dynamic is in the friendship; how they interact with my children and the rest of us. If possible, I invite their parents for dinner as well, and certainly my kids are not allowed to go over to someone else's house until I have had a conversation with my kids about the rules in their friend's house.

I will tell you a story of how this very thing has worked against me. One weekend, my son Mendy had a friend here. They took advantage of a moment of inattention, went on the Internet without our permission, and watched part of an episode of *South Park*, a show utterly inappropriate for children. Mendy's friend's father found out about it and forbid his son to come back to our house. I punished Mendy for disobeying, and refused to call the father to argue for a lift on the ban.

In fact, when I ran into him a few weeks later at a school function, I headed an uncomfortable moment off at the pass by saying, "Please don't apologize; you were absolutely correct, and I stand behind your decision one hundred percent. When your son is in someone else's home, you need to feel that someone will be supervising your son with the same attention that you would give him, and that's not what happened. I was not able to make sure that he didn't see something injurious to him, and you're absolutely right to be angry with me. You're right and I'm wrong."

If a friend is a bad influence, waste no time in moving to neutralize them. In what many people considered to be a radical move, I transferred my daughter Mushki from a school she enjoyed very much because I did not like a particular girl she had befriended there. This girl drank and had inappropriate relationships with boys. She was appealing to Mushki to help her "be better" and to stop these behaviors. As flattering as this may have been, Mushki, at fourteen, was in no position to act as a counselor to this girl. The school is a quality institution, as well as highly religious, but they didn't act quickly enough when I spoke to them, so I took matters into my own hands and transferred Mushki to another school in the middle of the year. She is flourishing there, thank G-d.

Protecting our children's innocence is just as important as protecting them physically. We should, of course, keep one eye on the outside dangers that threaten our children, but we must keep the other on the dangers that lurk in our video-game consoles, on their iPods, and in our own DVD players. I moved to protect Mushki, just as if she had been in physical danger. In my eyes, the threat is no less—so why would I do any less?

PROTECTION

CHAPTER THREE

*Honoring Our Children by
Protecting Them Emotionally*

A torn jacket is soon mended,
but hard words bruise the heart of a child.
—Henry Wadsworth Longfellow

The Bible is specific in insisting that we honor our parents, because we all have a natural tendency to resist authority, but there is no biblical commandment that we should show the same respect for our children.

It's surprising, isn't it? Perhaps no one envisioned a time when we would need to be told to do what seems to be the most natural thing in the world: to love our children, and to put them first. But when I look around me, I see that we now need this unwritten biblical commandment as much as the other. Of course we say that our children are the most important things in our lives, and that we'd do anything in our power for them. But unfortunately, that's not necessarily reflected in the way we behave toward them.

As we discussed in the previous chapter, we must protect our children from cultural influences that would damage them, in much the same way we are vigilant in protecting them physically. But we must also remember that we are the sole guardians of our children's emotional lives while they are children—and that the emotional experiences we give them when they are children will reverberate through the rest of their lives. So we cannot afford to overlook the tremendous influence that our own emotions and reactions—both positive and negative—can have on our children.

It may make you uncomfortable to look in this particular mirror, but it is essential that you do so. And you may scoff at some of the advice that follows: How can something as simple as gentle teasing or a carelessly forgotten promise have such a detrimental effect? But I believe that a parent who overlooks the effect of his behavior on his children is as great a hazard as a parent who ignores them.

Our own behavior is the single greatest determinant in how our children will develop emotionally.

We must never forget to treat our children like children; this is what it means to act like a parent. Think of how you behaved when your child was a baby. You washed your hands before feeding her, and then cradled her gently, as if you thought she might break. You shielded her eyes from harsh light, her ears from loud noise, her skin from even the slightest breeze. Did you imagine, as you supported that wobbly neck and squeamishly felt the soft spot in her skull, that you would one day curse in front of her— or worse, *at* her? Did you imagine that one day you would lie to her, which is all a broken promise really is? Of course you didn't. You knew better—just as you know better now.

It is only when we act like parents that we can truly protect our children emotionally.

As you read, I would invite you to remember that the majority of the dealings you will have with your children are pedestrian, everyday interactions. *This* is when we influence our children most. We have our greatest impact not during the stirring speeches we deliver as if in the locker room before a big game, but during the chats we have as we unload the dishwasher together and by the behavior we model when we are stuck in traffic. Your ability to elevate even these ordinary moments is at the heart of inspirational parenting.

PRESERVING EMOTIONAL TRANSLUCENCE

Children are born with an incredible emotional range, and they are able to access those emotions immediately. With very young children, there is absolutely no disconnect between what they feel on the inside and what they show on the outside. A two-year-old cries when he is hurt, laughs joyfully when he is delighted, whines for a cookie when he is hungry, yells when he is angry, and sleeps when he is tired. He is affectionate when cuddled, and afraid when he sees conflict between people he cares about. He feels everything, and expresses those feelings immediately and purely, without thinking of how he'll look or what other people will think of him.

That is emotional translucency, and it is a spectacular gift. Unfortunately, it is also a fleeting one—especially in a competitive society that tells us we have to toughen up to stay in the game. Teased enough, ignored enough, exposed enough, children learn to lie about what they're feeling. They learn that exposing themselves makes them vulnerable, so they hide what's going on inside. Eventually, they'll get to the stage most adults find themselves in, where they don't even *know* what they're feeling! When you camouflage your feelings, you become emotionally opaque, even to yourself.

I consider it to be the parents' job to help to preserve our children's emotional translucence so that they don't grow up to become brittle, insecure, emotionally inaccessible adults. This is why it is so important to treat our children with reverence and respect, not to tease them with something that humiliates them or say things that rob them of self-esteem. We must not break our promises to them, and we must not show them the worst aspects of our nature. Because if naïveté and trust are an invitation to be taken advantage of, then it will soon become advantageous for our children to become cynical and guarded. They will close up and steel themselves. They will toughen up and lose their childlike softness. And that is truly a tragedy.

As a first step in that direction, I think we need to shift our perspective so that we *see* our children differently and treat them differently as a result. The prosaic nature of our relationship with our children can color and even conceal their true natures for us, so that we begin to see them simply as the sticky little people who like to leave their toy trucks in the places we're most likely to trip over them. But we dare not forget that children are G-d's most treasured possessions, His little angels, and that they are entrusted to us to safeguard and protect.

In one of the most beautiful stories of the Bible, Moses

first encounters G-d at the burning bush. G-d says to him, "Take off your shoes." Why? Because the space that Moses was walking on was holy, and you cannot carelessly trample on hallowed ground. Our children are sacred, like that ground. They are the very embodiment of holiness; they have no sin. So we must be very careful to honor their purity, taking off our shoes so that we don't trample on them. The thought that my children are not mine, but of a divine nature, makes me feel infinitely more responsible to filter malign influences and preserve their incorruptibility. It also allows me to adopt an attitude of respect and reverence for my children, one that I think is essential.

PARENTING COMMANDMENT #1:
CONTROL YOUR OWN EMOTIONS

"Where is my Bluetooth headset?" I heard myself screaming. "Who moved it? I'm going to be late for my meeting; this is screwing up my whole day." The next morning, I saw my son Yosef getting ready for school. "Where is my red car?" he screamed. "This is ruining my whole day. Who moved my car?"

There is nothing so terrible as seeing the worst aspects of your character mirrored back to you by your children—and yet, this is precisely what happens when we fail to contain and control our own emotions. We too often explode at our family members because the bond between us is so close. Indeed, I know that my wife and children will not leave me if I yell at them—but does that make it right? No; it's an abuse of the very trust they have put in me.

A parent should model the very best aspects of human nature to their children.

Parents always say one thing when you ask them what they want for their kids: "I just want them to be happy." But happiness is the natural state of a child. The real objective is not to make our kids happy, but rather to not get in the way of their own natural happiness. *We're* the depressed, miserable ones—not our kids. And the only way they're going to stay happy is if we can manage not to spread our adult misery to them, like the contagion it is.

That's why it is so very important for parents to get a handle on our moods; we simply can't let things get to us. Josef looks to me for information and instructions on how to cope with complicated emotions; in this instance, all he saw was my childish inability to deal with the time constraints of an impending meeting and the frustration of losing the headset for my cell phone. Needless to say, it was not the lesson I had hoped to transmit.

Many of you will be familiar with the biblical commandment in the book of Deuteronomy to be happy on the days of G-d's festivals. When I was rabbi at Oxford, a smart student once asked me how G-d could command us to feel an emotion. "It makes perfect sense for G-d to command us how to act and what to do, because that's in our control, no matter how we feel. But emotions are not always in our control, so commanding us to be happy seems pretty unfair."

I thought about that question long and hard until I alighted on the obvious answer. "All G-d is asking us," I told this bright student, "is to be ourselves. We're all naturally happy, deep down. We're born happy. As kids, we smile and we play. But then we start growing up and the pressures of life slowly hit us, gradually sucking out the joy. First, there's the social pressure of wanting to be popular at school, and the academic pressure of nonstop work and exams. Then we get to college, where we have to fit in to a new environment without the comfort of home. Then we graduate and we have jobs, mortgages, irate bosses to deal with, not to mention the coffee stain on our pants. All of it takes its toll.

"What G-d is saying to us is this: 'Look, I get it. I understand that it's not easy to always be joyous as you tread water. But on my festivals, my joyous celebrations, I ask that you transcend the pressures of your life for a few days and thereby return to your natural self. Underneath all that frustration is the real you, the joyous you, the part of you that wants to live and breathe and be free. I give you these festivals so that you can return to your real self—even if just a few times a year—so that it's never lost to you.' "

Isn't this why people drink, to forget their problems so that they can laugh and be merry? It's not that a new person is created by the drink, but the alcohol evaporates the thick layer of care, so that the real person comes to the fore. The trick, of course, is to achieve that kind of transcendence without alcohol or any other external stimulant. Our challenge is learning to integrate the pressures of life, so that "the real us" isn't submerged under those pressures. We do this not just for ourselves but for our children.

And, as my student cogently pointed out, while our emotions may be out of our control, our actions are not. You may be tired or overwhelmed; indeed, your kids may be very annoying. You may *feel* like exploding. But that is no excuse for doing so.

"I couldn't help it; I just lost it," one of my friends said sheepishly to explain why he had hit the roof over something inconsequential like a spill in the backseat. "But you wouldn't 'lose it' with your boss, or with a cop at a traffic stop," I said to him. "Let's face it: you yell at the people you can yell at. If your kids could fire you or put you in jail, you'd be able to get yourself under control." He had to agree that this was true.

I often struggle with my temper. So although this commandment is one of the hardest for me to keep, I believe it is one of the most important, as well—for a number of reasons.

First of all, doing the television show has really opened my eyes to the perils of a short temper. In fact, one of the first things I noticed when we started doing the show was how *loud* the homes were. It sounds funny, doesn't it? But I couldn't believe how often voices were raised in anger. And it looks as bad as it sounds. Studying these families meant I was really watching for the first time, and could see how fundamentally grotesque a temper tantrum is. The face becomes distorted, spittle flies from the mouth—it looks monstrous. When you yell, you become a caricature of yourself, a human gargoyle, misshapen and ugly.

Yosef losing his cool over a toy car is embarrassing enough, but our children don't stop at mimicking our trivial blowups. In one of the episodes we taped for *Shalom in the Home*, the father who loved his family tremendously but seemed blind to how his behavior was influencing his offspring, repeatedly castigates his daughter for the disrespectful way she speaks to her mother. He goes so far as to call her a "devil child." We spent a little time in the editing suite, and came up with a "Greatest Hits" tape of his own: instance after instance of him yelling at his daughter *and* his wife. It turned out that we didn't need an exorcist for this devil child, just a father who was willing to take some responsibility and model better behavior, which this father, to his credit, has really strived to do.

While a fight with your spouse may seem inconsequential—the two of you may be perfectly capable of making up and moving on—remember that it rocks the very fundamental assumptions of your child's world. Seeing the two people he cares about most shouting at each other in what looks very much like hate is a devastating blow to everything he needs to be stable and secure. Think about that before you blow your top about who left the seat up, or which one of you forgot to put mustard on the shopping list. I, thank G-d, very rarely fight with my wife, but on a recent RV trip the long hours and close quarters got to both of us, and we ended up exchanging harsh words. The children were incredibly freaked out, and peace was not fully restored until I had apologized to my wife in front of my kids—and to the children themselves for frightening them. I scared myself that night. I could not believe I could frighten my children the way I did.

It is dangerous for our children to see us out of emotional control. They need to know that they live in a world that has order and meaning, and we're the people to give it to them. How can we deliver that with one hand, and then turn around and scream like a maniac about something trivial?

We need to be strong so that our children feel protected by us.

I will admit: I am sometimes tempted to get angry at an incompetent clerk, but I try to hold my tongue, not just because I want to treat everyone with respect, but because I want to model temperance to my children. I feel deep shame whenever I do something unbecoming in front of my children, and I apologize to them for it.

Sometimes I will go so far as to apologize for a *perceived* slight. Here's an example: Two of my daughters go to a school a long way away from our home, and there's no bus, so we hired a driver to take them in the morning. This man turned out to be an unlikable character; my daughters overheard him making fun of another girl at their school who has a serious physical disability. He was also profoundly unreliable, and it was this that provided the last straw: he told me on a Thursday afternoon that he was planning to take the whole next week off, effectively stranding my daughters during an exam period. I called him that night and told him we were going to find someone else, with the understanding that he would report to work for one final day.

In the car the next day, he told my daughters that I had spoken to him as if he were an animal. And although this was really not true, I called him, in front of my daughters, to apologize. My daughters were shocked! This was a bad guy—personally bad, and bad at his job, they reminded me. But his impression was that I had disrespected him, and I want my daughters to understand that I strive to be a gentleman always. That way they have no excuse not to act like ladies.

PARENTING COMMANDMENT #2: DO NOT BELITTLE

Rachel is one of my daughter's friends. She comes from a large family, most of them boys. In this family, everyone is a comedian; they revel in ribbing each other, sometimes quite harshly. You have no choice but to laugh it off; if you can't take the joke, you're a poor sport—and you'll be teased about that as well.

Rachel is struggling with a little bit of a weight problem. It's nothing to worry about—what my mother would call puppy fat—and it will disappear when she grows a couple of inches, as she will surely do in the next year. In her family, however, the extra pounds she's carrying are the source of much hilarity. For instance, one of her birthday presents this year was a pig-shaped cookie jar that makes snorting noises when opened, to the great amusement of everyone assembled.

As good-natured as everyone's intentions may be, I believe that Rachel's parents must stop participating in the teasing immediately, and that they must forbid her siblings to continue with it as well. There is, of course, an immediate danger: Rachel wouldn't be the first young girl to "correct" her weight problem by flirting with a dangerous eating disorder. But even if she manages to avoid that road, she will not escape from this teasing unscathed. Just as a cut on skin heals imperfectly, so will these cuts to her self-esteem and innocence leave thick, toughened, disfiguring scars.

Children and teenagers feel things very deeply, and that is the way it should be.

We do not want them to become calloused and hard, so that they can heartlessly laugh and shrug things off. And if we accidentally hit a nerve, we must apologize. I thoughtlessly teased one of my own daughters, who had shed some of her own childhood weight, by saying, "I liked you better when you were pudgy; you were nicer then." It never occurred to me that the few extra pounds had been a big deal to her; she was beautiful to me then, and she is beautiful to me now. But she was furious with me; she is not an angry girl, but she was very angry at that moment. "You have no idea how much I struggled, and how much I disliked the way I looked and felt when I was overweight," she yelled at me before storming off to her room. I was startled by the vehemence of her reaction, but the fault was all mine; I could only apologize for my insensitivity.

Of course, teasing isn't the only way we belittle our children. We do it when we minimize a child's problems, hopes, or fears—no matter how fanciful or bizarre they might seem to our adult minds. We do it when we criticize them publicly, from the sidelines of their sports games or at dinner with another family. We do it when we betray something that was told to us in confidence by using it against them in an argument later, or by telling someone else. If you want to be a part of your children's lives, you must be respectful of their emotions. If you prove yourself untrustworthy, you will not only hurt them immeasurably, but you will discover yourself locked out—and that hurts everybody.

PARENTING COMMANDMENT #3: KEEP YOUR PROMISES

During a very busy week, my youngest daughter, Baba, reminded me that I had promised to take her for ice cream. Just as dinner was ending, a friend called to ask me if I'd seen an article in a newsweekly that he thought might be of interest. I tore my office apart looking for the article, and when I found it, I got caught up in reading it and writing a response. I completely forgot my promise to Baba, and, in fact, pushed her off with further promises when she came to see where I was.

I happened to look up just as she was leaving the room, and caught a glimpse of the look on her face. In that moment, I gained a real understanding of something I had not fully grasped until that moment: breaking a promise to a child is a betrayal of the most fundamental and terrible kind. I had heard my spiritual mentor, the Lubavitcher Rebbe, say many times that we must be very careful not to break promises to a child, but I had not fully understood what he meant: that every broken promise is a lie, a weed in the Garden of Eden.

It's easy for an adult to say, "It's just ice cream! She can get some from the freezer! She'll forget all about it in five minutes." That might even be true. But children live in hope, and a promise is sacred to them. A promise is a bridge from the present to the future—more than that, a promise is a way for each one of us to play a role in controlling and building the future together. A promise says, "It will be, because we will make it so."

Promises sustain us. The Jews always believed with child-like innocence that G-d would keep His promise to return the Jewish people to the land of Israel. That promise sustained them. In the words of one great rabbi, "Even the cauldron of Auschwitz could not extinguish the flame of Jewish hope." Other nations have suffered the inevitable consequences of historical decline, but because the Jews believed what G-d said to them and held on to that promise, they survived even the Nazi persecution with their faith almost perversely intact.

It's too easy for us to break promises to our children,

especially when we dole them out right and left as pacifiers, bribes, and babysitters. But every broken promise blights hope, that most childlike of virtues. Every broken promise dismantles a child's ideal sense of the world, declaring it a place of chaos and uncertainty. It tells them that they have no control over what happens next. Worse, it makes a mockery of their beliefs, and tells them that their most deeply held convictions are inherently unsustainable.

Breaking promises to your children isn't just bad for their psyches, it's bad for your relationships with one another. Failing to live by your word not only breaks your children's hopes and hearts; it also makes you look dishonest and flimsy.

A broken promise makes you a liar instead of the hero you should be in children's eyes.

Children are right: promises should be sacred. Your word *should* be an indestructible bond. We should treat every commitment as if it were carved out of rock, and every canceled appointment, broken contract, and especially divorce should break our hearts. That is the best of humanity.

PARENTING COMMANDMENT #4:
SET BEHAVIORAL GROUND RULES

The biblical commandment is to *honor* one's parents, not to love them. This is because the Bible in its wisdom understands that a child may not always feel overt love for his parents. There will be times when he is angry, frustrated, bitter, even hostile, and he is entitled to his feelings. But this does not give him the right to treat his parents with disrespect. I am not a believer in the kind of routine abuse that takes place in American homes—the screaming and the backtalk, the cursing and the slammed doors. Parents should not yell at or verbally abuse their children, and I believe that children should be similarly respectful of their parents.

There are two reasons for this. The first is the obvious one: it is unpleasant and unnecessary, and sets a very unhappy tone in the house, robbing it utterly of "Shalom," peace. But the second reason to forbid—and I mean forbid—this kind of behavior in your home is to protect your children from the feeling that they have said something or done something unforgivable. In a sense, then, we set limits, not just so that our children can feel safe and protected from the outside world, but also safe and protected from themselves and emotions that we know to be detrimental.

One of the most shocking things I saw in the process of filming *Shalom in the Home* was a video that one of the fathers had shot of his three-year-old son having a tantrum. He had titled it "The Rage," and posted it on a Web site devoted to the boy, where it was one of the most popular items. To me, it was inappropriate to place it in the public domain and personally I found it difficult to even watch.

Three-year-olds will have tantrums, but it is a parent's job to engage with their children in those moments, to help them manage their anger. This father, although he loved his son with all his heart, stood silently by, filming. The episode lasts for about ten minutes: the child gets angrier and angrier at his father's lack of response to his anger, eventually working himself up into a complete frenzy while the father keeps the camera rolling. By the end, the child looks like he has been tortured.

The existence of this video is highly misguided, first because it is a violation of the privacy of a person. And indeed, we must be particularly vigilant to protect the fundamental rights of children, because they do not have the wherewithal to do it themselves. Children, too, have a right to privacy. But that is not the only thing that signals a failure to understand that the fundamental role of a parent is that of protector.

This father claimed that he had made the video as a learning tool, something he could show to his son. "Even if such a technique were likely to reach him," I asked, "don't you understand that when you allow him to experience that kind of anger, for that length of time, you allow him to do injury to himself? It's like revving an engine too much, or listening to music at too high a decibel level. You can do permanent damage, burning out the engine, your eardrums, or—in your son's case—his heart."

It is our job as parents to help our children negotiate the more complex emotions, and to protect them from the full strength of those emotions. You can't just stand by—filming!—as a child blows a gasket; you have a responsibility, whether they're right or wrong, to pacify them, to soothe them, to get them to calm down. Whether you choose to do that by holding them in your arms or stroking their head, or by explaining that you're going to give them a time-out if they don't stop screaming, is dependent on the child, the situation, and your own particular parenting style. But simply to stand by, further enraging the child with your own lack of engagement, mocking and inflaming him by filming his most private moment so that you can put it on a Web site, is wrong. We have to save our children from harming themselves in that way—not, certainly, egg them on for our filmmaking purposes.

My nephew used to have real problems with his mother, and their relationship was characterized by yelling. He would say mean things to her, in a highly disrespectful tone. I eventually interceded, and not for my sister's sake, but for his. I said to him, "The most horrible thing a human being has to live with is regret. It is a burden you can never unload. Trust me, when you are older and you see someone screaming at his mother, you will feel sick to your stomach and filled with the most terrible regret. The fights you now have with your mother will come flooding back to you, leaving you with the indelible taste of acid in your mouth. You won't forgive yourself. I want to prevent you from being haunted by this horrible feeling. Please listen to what I say, and stop yelling at your mother." It took a little while, but he did. Not, perhaps, before the damage was done, but he has at least had the opportunity to apologize to her and to work with her on healing their relationship, which, incidentally, has improved immeasurably, and he has become, today, a model son.

PARENTAL COMMANDMENT #5: DEMONSTRATE THE BEST POSSIBLE VERSION OF ADULTHOOD

Perhaps one of our biggest emotional responsibilities to our children is to *show* them that adulthood—while they should be in no hurry to get there—is also a time of privilege and respect, and not so far from the Garden of Eden as they might think. We can do that by modeling the best aspects of adulthood to them.

How careful are you about what you talk about in front of your children? My older, wiser friend Jeremy has always struggled financially. "My wife and I never talk about money or money problems in front of the kids," he told me. "We don't want the kids to know that we're struggling because we don't want money to be the principal thing on their minds." We cannot forget that our children are watching and listening, drawing important conclusions about life from the things that occupy and preoccupy us.

The way we live—not what we say—shows our kids what matters.

How many parents make the mistake of talking constantly about money in front of their kids—how much their friends have, and how much they lack? Before long, their kids have learned to value money above everything else, and they know to quantify everyone they meet in terms of how much they have. Jeremy's way is better.

I like to think that simply by living my life I am showing my children that there is much to love about "being a grown-up." It's not great to be an adult because you get to stay up as late as you want or to watch R-rated movies or have sex. It's great to be an adult because you can have satisfying work that makes the world a better place, work that you enjoy. It's great to be an adult because you can meet and marry a beautiful person who will be your partner in all of life's great and small adventures. It's great to be an adult because only then will you have the opportunity to parent wonderful children, who will enrich your life in myriad ways every day.

And there is no way to *tell* our children these truths that will speak to them as simply and effectively as our actions will.

Living a glorious and meaningful life is the best inspiration we can give our children.

About once a month, my family goes to the grave of the late Lubavitcher Rebbe, Rabbi Menachem Schneerson, who died in 1994. We don't go to worship him; Jews don't worship anyone except G-d. We don't go because I feel that I need an intermediary in my relationship with G-d; Jews believe that every one of us has a direct line. And I can always listen to some of the rebbe's speeches on tape or read his writings if I want to be reminded of what he said or believed.

I go to his grave because standing there reminds me of how he *lived*. His was a life of charity and scholarship, of wisdom and supreme generosity, and the example of his life inspires me to aspire to those things in my own life. When I stand at his grave, I am reminded of how rousing it was to see him living a life of devotion to G-d and other people. Nothing inspires like action, and it is the rebbe's example that I summon when I strive to be the best human being possible, not just because it's the right thing to do, but because of the example it sets for my children.

I don't flinch from being held to this higher standard of behavior—in fact, I aspire to it.

I strive always to be a better man because I want my children to see in me not just a father, but a hero.

I have myself been lucky in this regard; I was raised by my mother, who is—by all standards—an extraordinary person. Although she struggled, financially and otherwise, to raise five children on her own, there was always room at her table. There are so many examples of her generosity and hugeness of spirit, but I will give one that I heard during my last trip to visit her in Florida, because I think it shows not just how generous she is, but how important she thinks it is to preserve other people's dignity—a quality I try to emulate every single day.

At Shabbos dinner one night at her home, a rabbi she knows took me aside and told me this story: "I have devoted my life to teaching children. It is a rewarding and blessed life, but the remuneration is poor. This is something I would not mind if it was not for my wife, who is a wonderful woman. Last year, I was desperate to think that I would not be able to buy her anything special for our twenty-fifth wedding anniversary. I never said a word to your mother—I have no idea how she found out—but a few days before the anniversary, she stopped by our house with a beautiful gold necklace in a velvet box, and refused to accept payment of any kind. She accepted my thanks, but has forbidden the topic between us since."

My mother's singular goodness was a source of inspiration to me every single day growing up. She made adulthood look like an honorable state. And I can think of no greater tribute to her than to honor her by emulating her actions as her son, in order that my own children see my example and feel inspired by it. My kids know I'm not the smartest guy; they know I'm not the richest or the most handsome. But I hope that they think of me as a good man, and that they see my struggles, both the ones I win and the ones I do not, as inspiration. I want them to look forward to their adulthood, and all the glories that adulthood brings—just not before they are ready for it.

Love

CHAPTER FOUR

The Power of Unconditional Love— and the Danger of Raising Kids Without It

> The greatest gift a parent can give a child
> is unconditional love. As a child wanders and strays,
> finding his bearings, he needs a sense of absolute love
> from a parent. There's nothing wrong with tough
> love, as long as the love is unconditional.
> —George Herbert Walker Bush

Let me ask you a question:

Do you love your children?

Of course you do; I know you do. Indeed, for many of us, it is an emotion so enormous that we barely have words to describe it. I was unprepared for the wave of emotion that hit me when my eldest daughter was placed in my arms for the first time, and am happy to report that the feeling is undiminished (if anything, it has intensified) with every year that has passed. The same is true of the seven brothers and sisters who have come since.

But something has gone wrong. We are raising a generation of insecure, unhappy children, children who feel unloved, and who are driven by that lack of love into chasing affirmation from other sources, like rampant materialism, drug and alcohol abuse, and sexual promiscuity. Clearly, there is a disconnect between what we feel and what we show; what we say and what we do; and I believe that this disconnect is behind many of the perils that threaten the happiness and stability of the American family.

Our objective must be to make sure that our children always feel loved and cherished. Above all else, we have to make them feel like they matter, and we have to give them attention without asking them to earn it. I consider this to be one of our most important charges as parents, and yet it seems to have fallen off our agendas. Let's be honest: children today have taken a backseat to their parents' careers and leisure time. We've outsourced our responsibilities the way we've outsourced American jobs. And we've allowed other support systems—including our children's friends—to take our place at the center of their lives, with truly devastating consequences.

In this chapter, I will show you why it's so important that you—and the unconditional love that *only you* can provide—be squarely in the center of your children's lives. And then I will show you how you can put yourself back there, where you belong.

THE INSECURITY TREADMILL

Let us first look at why unconditional love is so very important—for everyone, but especially for our children.

Most Americans are safe from the tribulations that affect much of the world. We live in a glorious democracy; our drinking water is safe; food is inexpensive and plentiful; our health care system is unrivaled. Why, then, are we so miserable?

Because we feel like we don't matter.

At our very core, there is emptiness, a lack of conviction about our own worth. We think we don't matter, so we buy bigger and bigger trinkets—cars, houses, diamonds—to prove that we do, but none of the junk we acquire satisfies us for long. We think we're unlovable, so we buy designer handbags and chase youth by going under the plastic surgeon's knife, but it's all to no avail; there will always be someone younger and better-looking, and even a completely unlined face won't iron out the wrinkles in our soul. Look at the celebrity culture! Our idols are people who have turned their insecurities into an art form, like Donald Trump, people who despite their fortunes won't rest until everyone in the world acknowledges their accomplishments.

This is the insecurity treadmill, a subject I have written about at great length in my book *The Private Adam*. It is a trap that keeps us dissatisfied with ourselves and the blessings we have, perpetually grasping after a brass ring that will always be just out of our reach.

Now why, with all our comparative wealth and advantages, are Americans so fundamentally insecure? I believe the answer is a lack of love and attention in our childhood.

If our parents haven't made it clear to us that we're important and worthy of love, how can we ever convince ourselves that it's true?

Love may come second to protection in the PLANT parenting method, but loving our children unconditionally is really part of protecting them. Love is the very backbone of human development, and being loved makes a child feel secure and confident—indeed, it is the only thing that will. When parents invest time and attention in a child, that child feels valuable and worthy at his very core, but a child who feels secondary in his parents' hearts will always feel secondary in his own life.

When that chain of transmitted love is broken, the children grow up broken as well, and go on to raise broken children of their own, and so on, and so on, and so on. Sure, you can heal yourself from parental neglect, but you start out behind the eight ball. I know; I have counseled hundreds of people with broken lives, and the common denominator with nearly all of them was neglectful parenting.

But that insecurity need not rule our lives. It's not too late for us, and it's certainly not too late for us to break the cycle so that our children can live happy, healthy, and productive lives without always feeling that they can't measure up. We can heal ourselves, and our children, through inspirational parenting. When we put our families first, and devote our time and energy to the things in our lives that really do matter, we can step off the insecurity treadmill and begin to feel like heroes in our own homes. And in so doing, we can ensure that this pathological insecurity is not the legacy we leave to our children.

LOVING YOUR KIDS—NO MATTER WHAT

Not only must our children know they are loved, they must know they are loved *unconditionally*. We must make them understand that their value is intrinsic to them—even if they don't have perfect skin, perfect grades, or perfect behavior. They have to understand, at the very root of their being, that they don't have to do anything to earn our love, or to keep it.

Our children were born worthy of perfect love, and they will have it for their entire lives, simply because they are.

Nothing they can do can make us love them more—because how can you increase something that's already infinite? And nothing they do can weaken our love, either, because it's harder than diamond, the bond more impenetrable than kryptonite.

When your children know they have your unconditional love, they can keep it with them forever.

I don't think we fully realize how important this is to convey to our children—and how easily their faith in that bond is shaken. On a trip to Washington, DC, I put my daughter Chana in charge of our expensive new digital camera. Two hours later, it was nowhere to be found; she had left it in the hotel lobby, and it had disappeared. I was angry at Chana for her carelessness, especially since I saw it as part of a pattern of inattention. I told her how irresponsibly she had behaved and how disappointed I was in her, and although I could see how dejected she was, I was not in a frame of mind to bolster her confidence.

Six months passed, and the family was on an RV trip in Nashville, Tennessee. I deliberately put Chana in charge of the camera; I wasn't going to give up on her learning responsibility! But without her knowing, my wife took the camera and walked ahead. Panicking, Chana searched the entire RV and could not find it. We waited at Nashville's perfect copy of the Parthenon for almost an hour for her and my eldest daughter, Mushki, to turn up. When they did, Chana had tears in her eyes. Mushki said, "Chana couldn't find the camera, and was afraid to come here because she didn't think you wanted her without it."

It was one of my lowest moments as a parent. Had I really failed in making my daughter feel loved? Could she really believe that I would only want her company if she returned with some unimportant piece of electronics? That night, I sat all my kids down in the RV and said, "In general, I'm a pretty happy person. G-d has given me so many blessings! But if anything were to ever happen to one of you, I would never know happiness again. I would soldier on, for Mommy and for all the other children's sake. I would get up in the morning, but I would never want to. I would still smile, but every smile would be fake. My world would be permanently dark. To the extent that there is light in my world, it's because you came into it. Before you were born, I did not know what life was and I did not know what love was. I love all of you more than anything in the world. I love you when you succeed, I love you when you fail. I love you when you find gold mines and when you lose cameras. There is nothing in the world you can do to increase my love for you, and there is nothing you can do to lose even an iota of it. You are the light of my life, and without you, nothing else is valuable. If I have ever made any of you feel any different, then I am sorry, and I apologize with all my heart. And I hope you will forgive me."

They heard what I was saying, but this event had a profound

effect on me as well. It provided me with a litmus test for my own reactions: no misdeed is serious enough that it is worth making my children think they're not loved.

We're all guilty, to some extent, of making our children feel that our love is based on what they do as opposed to who they are. We're so achievement-oriented ourselves—of course it seeps into our relationships with our children. Many of us learned this from our very own parents. I myself harbor the scars of insecurity because of my distant relationship with my father when I was young. After my parents' divorce, my father not only lived far away from us but felt driven by his own poor childhood to succeed financially, so that no family member of his would ever have to be poor again—but unfortunately, the message his kids got was that business came first. He never intended that. Indeed, he loved us unconditionally. But we didn't always see that.

I ended up comfortable on the outside but impoverished on the inside. To get my father's attention as a child and young man, I felt that I needed to have something positive to report: good grades, a good job, meeting and marrying a good woman. Now, I'm thirty-nine years old and I still feel the need to get his attention through my accomplishments. I got a TV show, or I am publishing another book, or that my kids have become certified scuba divers. But this year, on my birthday, I called my father and I said to him, "I want you to know that I love you very much and I consider myself the son of a great man. But I need a father, and you need a son; we both need the un- conditional love that we can only get from one another. It's not something that you can get from your business associates, and it's not something that I can get from mine." Our relationship has improved immeasurably and I am well aware that the best way to heal myself is by finding that sense of unconditional validation.

We must also be careful not to project our own needs and desires onto our children, living through them and robbing them of lives of their own. We did a very disturbing TV show that painfully demonstrates this point. The mother was estranged from her own parents because she is a lesbian and had chosen to have a child through artificial insemination. Her parents' rejection still rankles, and she has responded by molding her daughter into the perfect student—"See? You think my daughter's cursed by G-d, but how bad can she be? She is a perfect, straight-A student!" The girl is a prodigy with the grades to match, but she is also very unhappy and virtually incapable of relaxing and having fun like the child she is. The only thing that gives her satisfaction is doing well in school.

This mother, a remarkable woman in so many respects, has inadvertently made her daughter feel that the gift of her love is conditional on externals like grades and college board scores. She has virtually guaranteed her daughter a seat on the insecurity roller coaster. To her credit, in the wake of our show, she made great changes and her daughter is much, much improved as a result. The pressure to "do well" is endemic in our society. My daughter recently told me about a girl in her class who hyperventilated until she nearly passed out when she received a B on a test.

Our children must understand, now and forever, that they're not loved because of how smart they are, or how fast they can throw a ball, or how polite they are. The unconditional love our children get from us is the foundation upon which their characters are built, so that foundation must be rock-solid and unyielding. Then they will pursue knowledge because they are curious and love to know, not because they want to get into Princeton. It is time for us to reverse the existing equation: our children should want to achieve because we have given them a tremendous sense of self-worth and they want to live up to their full potential—not because they sense that the carrot of Mommy's love will be whisked away if they don't.

Our children should want to achieve because they already have our unconditional love, not in order to earn it.

Instead of making my love conditional, I choose to parent inspirationally. My daughter Shterny struggled in school this past year; one day I got calls from three separate teachers to report her inattention in class and tardiness with her assignments. That night I called her into my office, and the excuses started before she was through the door. "I know why you want to talk to me, Tatti, and I'm sorry; I know I've been slacking off, and I'm going to try harder and do better, I promise."

I interrupted her, and said, "Shterny, stop. Lift your eyes and look at me. You think you know why I called you in here, but you don't. I called you into my office to tell you, simply, that I love you. And by the way, now that you know that I love you, in addition, I want you to focus more and try harder at school. But that's not why I called you in. I called you to tell you that you're my sweet baby girl, and I adore you. I did get calls from three of your teachers this afternoon. But if a thousand teachers called me to tell me how poorly you were doing in school, I would still love you. And if you won the Rhodes scholarship tomorrow, I wouldn't love you any more. My message to you is simply that you are the light of my life. I called you in to my office tonight because I wanted to tell you that.

"And by the way, please give your studies a little more attention." It is Shterny's responsibility to pursue learning because she loves knowledge. And it is my responsibility as her father to love her, no matter what. That did not mean that I didn't monitor Shterny over the next few days and make her do her homework and study. It did mean that I did it all in the spirit of unconditional acceptance.

You can never love your child too much. The love you feel, show, and share with your child is with him forever, the strong foundation upon which he will form his character. And in the next chapter, I will show you how to make sure that the message of love you're transmitting is being received.

Love

Chapter Five

Why Is Our Love Getting Lost in Translation?

Hugs can do great amounts of good—especially for children.
—Diana, Princess of Wales

Nothing can replace the unconditional love we provide our children. But I see that many children aren't getting that message of unconditional love from their parents, in the same way most of us didn't get it from our parents. And we're all a little bit messed up as a result—not as secure as we otherwise might be, and certainly not as happy. Are there really no parents who love unconditionally? No; in most cases, the problem isn't a lack of love, but an inability to *show* that love.

It's not enough to love your kids—you have to *show* them you love them.

An emotion that is never expressed may as well have never been felt; what we feel in our hearts must be articulated by our lips and practiced by our hands.

Why did your own parents fail to show you, and tell you, how much you mattered? Maybe they were working too hard, or struggling with a bad marriage. Many of us, myself included, grew up in a household where a TV blared in the living room in place of real conversation in the kitchen. Many of us felt more comfortable with the families we saw every week on TV than we did with our own, and we show the scars as a result.

We know better than to repeat the injuries we sustained. I believe we now have to take steps to clear the obstacles that stand in the way of our children's full experience of the power of unconditional parental love. This is the way to step off the treadmill forever; the more love you show, the more important your child will feel—and the less she will need to seek affirmation elsewhere, whether from her friends, illegal substances, or in a sexual partner's eyes.

All you have to do is show your children that they're loved, and, as you'll see in the pages that follow, it's amazing how easy it is to make them feel that way.

#1: TELL THEM

Our love for our children burns so brightly in our hearts that we assume they know how we feel. But that's not a safe assumption to make. There's no substitute for hearing the words "I love you"; after all, you assume that your spouse loves you, but doesn't it warm your heart to hear it?

I tell my kids that I love them many times a day. And this isn't a pat, absentminded "love you" as I drop them off at school. I isolate specific qualities about my children and compliment them on those qualities. "I love spending time with you because of the artistic way you see the world." "I love you because you have an incredibly good heart. You're always volunteering to help around the house." "I love spending time with you because you are such a refined young lady."

Yes, sometimes they giggle and ignore me; sometimes they tease me, calling me corny. I don't care, and I tell them so. I'm not going to stop loving them, or demonstrating my affection, no matter what they say or how embarrassing they find it. I won't capitulate to their evolving cynicism; instead, I throw myself under its wheels, in an attempt to slow it down. Plus, it makes me feel good to tell them—and I can tell, underneath all that adolescent scoffing, that they like to hear it, too.

Whenever my kids come home from school, I stop them and *make* them come over to me and give me a kiss and a hug, whether they want to or not, and whether they feel like it or not. And it cuts both ways; when they come home, I try to always interrupt what I am doing—talking on the phone, writing this chapter—to greet them, hug them, and kiss them. I will purposely make a point of showing them that their appearance at home has caught my attention and inter-rupted my work, because *they come first*. And they know that I work to give them a good life, but they are the light of my life, not my work.

There are other ways to tell our children that we see what they do, who they are, and love them for it. Have you noticed how kids seek our approval? They are always showing us the pictures they've drawn, how they dive into the swimming pool, how they cleaned up their room—all in an effort to so-licit a compliment. Kids are bottomless pits for affection. They have no fear, when they are young, of showing their vulnerability. Unlike us adults, they don't feel the need to feign strength and independence.

But my friend Paul, a father of three, believes that unearned praise ruins children. He also believes in truth at all costs. So if his kids hit the baseball badly, he tells them so. If their picture looks more like a tornado than it does like a house, he tells them that, too.

I couldn't disagree more. I lavish compliments on my children, and when I'm done, I pour on some more. To Paul, I say that we are the source of our children's self-esteem, and they need to know we honor and value their contributions, no matter what they look like. And really, when we compliment the misshapen monster they assure us is a picture of ourselves, we're not lying; we're paying tribute to a higher truth. Because it's we who don't see. Everything a child does is magical and wondrous; if his picture looks awful to you, it's because you are looking with corrupt adult eyes, confined by a rigid definition of beauty rather than the innocent and unlimited expression of a child's inner world.

I know parents who worry about spoiling their kids with compliments, but that's not how children get spoiled. You spoil a child when you fail to make and enforce rules—which, when you think about it, is really complimenting them for *bad* behavior. As long as you are maintaining a high set of standards for your children's behavior, as I try to do, why shouldn't you praise them for their successes? Making note of their good behavior and good works is just as important as disciplining them for the bad.

It is especially important to tell our children we love them when they are testing the limits of that love. I learned something from a young mother when her daughter was acting like a particularly terrible two-year-old. She had just thrown her breakfast plate to the ground in a fury after seeing that her toast had been cut in a way she didn't like, and she was getting a time-out. As the woman put her daughter in the playpen, she kissed her head and said, "I'm very angry with you for throwing your food because that's not the way we act even when we're upset, but I want you to know that I love you every second of every minute of every day, even when I'm angry with you."

The baby still howled, but I was struck by how compassionate the young mother's gesture was, and it is something I try to incorporate every time I have to discipline one of my children. They may still howl, but I know they hear me. It can be hard to tell a sulky, rebellious teenager that you love him, especially after he's borrowed the car without asking and then totaled it. But I think it is essential to tell our kids we love them, especially when the relationship is under extreme duress and we have to act as disciplinarian. Knowing that the punishment we mete out is because of—not in spite of—our love sustains and strengthens them. And it serves as a reminder for us as well: as we've already discussed, it can be hard to discipline our children. Remembering that we do so out of love can help us to remain consistent and firm.

#2: SHOW IT

It is chilling to realize that there are some infants in the world who die not because they don't receive sufficient nourishment or warmth, but because they are not touched.

Everyone likes to be held and hugged, but scientists are now discovering that physical contact with the people we care about can lower stress-related symptoms like high blood pressure, increase our immune function, and relieve the perception of pain. In short, there is no substitute for tactility.

And yet, there is all too little overt affection in the American home. I hear it over and over again: "I know my father loved me, but he didn't know how to show it." "My mother wasn't raised in a demonstrative home, so she wasn't all that demonstrative with us." It's nice to make excuses for your parents. But in the final analysis, there are no excuses. Showing our children love in the most tangible, physical way is important, and we cannot forget it.

We cuddle and kiss our children endlessly when they're tiny. They love nothing better than to burrow up close to us for a story or a tickle, and they don't need a researcher to tell them that a kiss and a hug have remarkable healing properties. But when they reach a certain age, it's as if an iron gate comes down, so that the handshake and pat on the back we exchange with our casual business acquaintances starts to look like an intimate physical relationship compared to what we have with the people we're supposed to be closest to.

I think this is why so many parents make the mistake of giving all their affection to their younger children—they'll take it! It's much more gratifying to show affection toward a toddler who will giggle uproariously when you make smacking kissy noises on his tummy than his grumpy teenaged sister. But even when she's the one doing the rejecting, she'll feel ignored and jealous if her parents focus their affection on her little brother. I too have been guilty of this: our family is neatly divided into two age groups—the four older kids, ages thirteen to seventeen, and the four younger kids, ages eleven to six months. I often find myself more openly affectionate toward the little ones, simply because they're so responsive. The older ones take a lot more work!

But it is work you have to do. We saw this on our TV show when we worked with a family who had three teenage kids from previous marriages and a two-year-old from the current one. The father was a warm and handsome man who found that his teenage kids were forever running out to be with friends, so he turned all his affection on the baby. We were able to show him tape that brought to light the mistake he was making: he'd walk in the door and go straight to pick up the baby, who would spend the rest of the night on his hip. He hugged and kissed and cooed at the baby, while ignoring his teenagers as much as they ignored him. He was, in my opinion, preempting the rejection.

The older kids needed to be brought back into the fold of his love, but he was afraid to take the risk, so he took the easy way out. Babies love to be held, so he held the baby. Once this father saw what he was doing, he easily understood how destructive it was, and it inspired him to change the situation. In the space of the few days we spent together, his relationship with his older children greatly improved, and he has since told me that his teenage children have begun to confide in him in all sorts of ways.

I take an inordinate amount of pride in the fact that my daughters are daddy's girls. What does that mean? For me, it means that a girl knows that she's the apple of her father's eye, foremost in his mind. She feels validated by the relationship, and doesn't have to compete for his attention. It means that she doesn't need—and isn't open to—the false manipulation of some teenaged boy, because she has confidence and gets the affection and attention she needs from a more wholesome source. And it means that later, she will judge the men she dates by the honorable standard her adoring and respectful father has set.

In a bit of advice for which I will always be grateful, I asked a child-rearing expert on my radio show how I can ensure that my five daughters will be daddy's girls. She said simply, "Hug and kiss them, constantly, and make them reciprocate." And that is exactly what I do. The first thing they do when they come in the door, before they drop their bags or get snacks or pet the dog, is to give me a hug and a kiss, and to get one in return, even if I'm in the middle of a telephone conversation. After a while, it becomes second nature.

Daddy's girls are not born. They are made—by their fathers.

I know it's unusual for teenage daughters to kiss their father without complaining, and I frankly don't care if it embarrasses them. When I drop them off at school, I tell them, "I don't care who sees, and I don't care if you're mortified. I don't care if you're a social pariah and never have another friend as long as you live. You're going to kiss me before you get out of this car." They giggle and groan and roll their eyes, but they do it—and so far, none of them has paid with her popularity. And if they do, who cares? Being close to their father is much more important than being close to their friends.

I heard Ron Kuby, the New York radio host, tell his listeners about going to see the fourth Harry Potter movie. In his review of the film, he mentioned that he and his wife had taken his thirteen-year-old daughter and some of her friends to see the movie—and he noted that the teenagers ("of course") sat separately, in a different part of the theater. I was shocked by this—these kids were embarrassed to be seen with someone's parents, as if going to the movies as a family was some bizarre ritual practiced only by cannibals. Kuby, a highly respected legal expert, told the story with absolutely no sense of irony; as an American parent, he had been conditioned to view showing affection, or a desire to be around his daughter in public and around her friends, as something that might embarrass her. Amazingly, we parents capitulate to such nonsense. What's next? Being ashamed to show affection to our spouses? How has love become something to be ashamed of in America?

Don't tolerate it. Jonah, a visitor who came to our home for the Sabbath, noticed the physical affection my kids show to their parents and expressed surprise. "I can't remember the last time my daughter kissed me," he said. "Kiss her," I said. "I can't," he replied. When pressed, he admitted that she had very hurtfully wiped her cheek after his last attempt, a rejection that had wounded him deeply. Nothing could induce him to try again.

Jonah found it humiliating to be rejected by his daughter. I'm surprised to find how prevalent this is. Of course, parents have feelings too. But to abandon best parenting practices (like showing physical affection to your children) because your feelings are hurt is a serious abnegation of your responsibility. You must persevere, even if you are greeted with the utmost resistance. You must put pride aside, and be the parent.

This can be difficult, especially when the rejection takes place over a sustained period of time, but let me reassure you: your children want you to make the effort. No matter how cold and alienated and rejecting they seem, deep inside they want you to reach out to them, coaxing them out of their shell. Everyone does, but children especially. Your love, and the manifestations of that love, are something they cannot live without. So do not allow yourself to be dissuaded from giving them that love, no matter what they say or do.

I was in a taxi recently, and asked the driver about his family. He had last spoken to his adult children at Thanksgiving—and the time before that had been the previous Thanksgiving. I pressed him for more information: why wasn't he talking to his children? "They don't want to talk to me," he said. "Who asked them?" I replied. "You are their father, their only father. It is a spiritual bond rooted in biology, but one that has the possibility of being so much more. Being out of touch with them causes you pain; of course it does. It's a reversal of the natural order of things; we should be close to our families. But calling them once a year isn't going to melt the ice that has built up around their hearts. Why aren't you making more of an effort to get close to them?"

The answer, of course, was that he was afraid of being rejected. "They're angry at me," he said. "I'm afraid of what they'll say."

"Well, screaming and yelling may not be what you want to hear, but it's a step forward—at least then they'll be showing strong feelings to you," I replied.

"I'm worried they'll tell me to stop calling," he said.

"Fine. Then you'll write a letter, telling them you're sorry for your absence and want to be a father to them now. You can push through the resistance of their anger, but you will have to make the effort."

No matter how severe the alienation, I know one thing: if you show enough love to your kids, you will get through to them. We cannot afford to allow our own foolish pride to stand between us and the relationship we desire with our children.

#3: SPEND TIME WITH THEM

Rabbi Shneur Zalman, a genius scholar and the first Lubavitcher Rebbe, had a son, Rabbi Dovber, who was another great scholar, famous for his powers of concentration.

Rabbi Dovber was studying the Torah when his infant son began to cry, but he did not move from his books, so the great rebbe went to change the baby and soothe him back to sleep. When he was done, he came to the room where his son was studying, so lost in concentration that he hadn't even heard the infant cry.

"There is something very flawed about your whole religious experience—so much, indeed, that you should do long contemplation about how you can correct it," the rebbe said.

"Why do you say that?" asked his bewildered son.

The rebbe explained: "Your studies are worthless if you cannot hear the cry of a child. In fact, the ultimate point of your study should be to be attentive to that cry."

Sound familiar? In frenetic, twenty-first-century America, showing our children that we love them can simply mean making enough room to accommodate them in our lives, and that means not allowing the *urgent* things in life to trump the more *important* ones. Let me explain. Let's say I sit down to read a child a story, and my cell phone rings. I know what I'm doing is important—bonding with my son, teaching him to love the written word, even the fact that I'm relaxing myself, for the first time all day—but the call is *urgent*. If I don't pick it up, I'll miss it. So I take it, and when I'm done, I remember that there's something absolutely essential that I need to see on the news, and when that's done I realize that the gym will only be open for another hour. There will always be another time for a story, right? So I go—choosing the urgent over the important.

The damage I've done is immeasurable, especially if this is a pattern of behavior that I repeat over and over again. Ballet recital? Well, this conference is going to run long, and I'm sure my little girl will understand. Family dinner? My boss wants me to entertain the new clients, and we really want this account. Before long, the most important things in your life feel like they're at the bottom of your list of priorities. The message I've sent to that child, waiting for his story, is this: "You're not important. Sally from Sales is important, the news is important, my abs are important. These things matter. You do not."

The reality, of course, is the opposite. All those things are distractions from the real prize. They don't matter, in the long run, but our children really do, and they need us to tell them, in word and action, and over and over again, that they do. If we don't, they will find a way, in word or action, to tell us how much they suffer as a result.

A businesswoman I know told me a story that broke my heart. For Mother's Day, her five-year-old daughter's kindergarten class made drawings of their mothers and collected them into small books, sewn together with yarn. When my friend opened her book, she saw that *in every single picture* her daughter had drawn her with a cell phone pressed to her ear. It was a sobering wake-up call for her, and one I am happy to report she heard. Today when her cell phone rings, she presses "ignore" on her phone, not on her daughter.

In accommodating the "urgent," we compromise the truly important.

The irony, of course, is the number of elderly parents who trampled on the important during their urgent years and are now sitting in Miami or Tucson, wishing they had something more fulfilling to sustain them. How can we expect our children to put family life first if we consistently show them how low it is on our own list of things to do?

When parents call to ask if I can counsel their children, I always tell them I would be happy to, but only after an initial consultation with the whole family. When they show up, regardless of the nature of the problem at home, I always try to determine how much time the family spends together as a family. It's usually very little, and the story is always the same: We're busy people; the kids are overscheduled; there simply aren't enough hours in the day. Unfortunately, I can't accept that as an answer; there is always a way. We live in a free country and we all end up doing what we *want* to do. They don't need me or any other counselor, I tell them. They need *you*.

Let me give you an example from my own life. My daughter Shterny is a very good daughter, and an even better sibling. When she began to do poorly in school, I looked at the time we spent together and realized I had no one but myself to blame. I hadn't been focused on her, and I certainly wasn't giving her the time she needed. One night, before an important test, I was scheduled to appear on *Larry King Live*, but Shterny needed my help to study—so I brought her with me. Instead of preparing my own notes or reviewing my most powerful arguments, I studied with Shterny. I quizzed her in the back of the car they sent for me, and our study session went all the way to the greenroom, until the production assistant came in to tell me I was on.

I wanted Shterny to understand that she comes first. *She* is the most important thing in my life, not a television appearance, or Larry King, or the people watching his show. She is more important than my career, or my book sales, or my own television show. It's a good thing for her to see that I have a demanding job that I enjoy, but only if she knows that she comes first in my life, with only her mother and G-d preceding her.

We show people they matter by prioritizing them, by putting them first.

And when your kids know they come first, amazing things happen. They begin to accord themselves a whole new level of respect—and this in itself makes for a whole new form of inspirational parenting. Shterny gave her studies her full attention because *I* was giving them—and more important, her—my full attention. She did well on her exam. More important, I felt much closer to her than I had, and that was ultimately a lot more satisfying than getting great feedback on a television appearance.

This is one of the reasons I so enjoy observing the Sabbath. Monday through Friday, I am submerged by the urgent as the phone rings, the BlackBerry buzzes, and pages spew out of the printer and the fax. But as an Orthodox Jew, all those urgencies fall away on the Sabbath. I can't answer those phone calls, turn on the television, or transact any business at all. For twenty-four hours, nothing urgent exists—just the important: my wife, my kids, the guests surrounding me at our table, and G-d Almighty, the source of all those blessings, who hovers over the whole experience.

Even during the rest of the week, I don't accept excuses from myself about why I can't spend time with my family. I travel a lot, it's true, but I look for ways to stay in touch even when I travel. For instance, I usually bring a camcorder to record the places I visit, the lectures I give, the panels I participate in, so that I can show them to the kids when I get back. When I go to film my TV show, I call the kids at night, pack them around the speakerphone, and tell them about the family we're meeting, their unique situation, and how we're trying to help. I have, on occasion, even brought along a book of theirs along with my own books, to read to them. Of course it's not as good as being there, but it's much, much better than nothing at all.

Get creative! The technology that makes it so easy for work to reach us at home can also make it easy for home to reach us when we must work. For instance, a TV producer I know got a scanner for his computer; his kids e-mail him the homework they're having trouble with, and he helps them with it from his hotel room. It's a great investment. Another television executive I know uses webcams to "have dinner" with her kids when she's on the road, as she must sometimes be; she orders her lunch from room service, and they all sit around the virtual table together, interrupting each other and telling jokes as if they were all on the same continent. Again, there is *no* complete substitute for being there. And you have to minimize travel and prioritize your kids. But these contingencies do provide the next best thing.

Giving life to your child isn't a one-time event; it's an ever-renewing process that takes place every time you show him love. And, like the snack pack you stick in his pocket to sustain him physically through the course of the day, the goodness of your love will sustain him emotionally through both the dark patches and the glory days ahead.

It will also sustain you. If one of my books is successful, I feel great—for a minute. But then I begin worrying about the next one, and whether I will have anything interesting or original to say, and whether anyone will care. On the other hand, when I know I have accorded my children the position they deserve in my heart, and when I see them basking in the warmth of my love, I feel like the biggest success in the world.

For everyone's sake, be generous with your love. It's an endlessly renewable resource, and a powerful one.

Love

CHAPTER SIX

*The Dangers of Conditional Love: How Friends
Are Ruining the American Family*

The best way to keep children at home is to make the home
a pleasant atmosphere and let the air out of the tires.
—Dorothy Parker

When our television show was shooting with a family in Pennsylvania, one of their friends volunteered to drive me back to my hotel because she wanted to talk about how she could repair her relationship with her daughter. Her daughter was hardly ever home—and when she was, she barely seemed present. She never talked to her parents about anything of importance, and when pressed would give only the most perfunctory answers, although her mother could hear her talking for hours on the phone with her friends. She said it was like living with a ghost, and a rude one at that.

Another woman whose family appeared on our show told me how hurt she was when she bumped into another mother from her daughter's school at the supermarket one afternoon and heard that her daughter had begun dating a new boyfriend. "Can you imagine the humiliation I felt, that some stranger knew more about my daughter's personal life than I did?" she asked me.

What I am about to say may be controversial, but I think there are few dangers as great as the ones we invite over for playdates on the weekends: our children's friends. Not the friends themselves, perhaps (although sometimes, they're threat enough!), but the insidious idea that friendships deserve the same energy and commitment as family life. At the heart of this idea is the dangerous belief that the love and admiration our children get from their peers is a viable replacement for the unconditional love they receive from their parents and their siblings. It is not.

The conditional love and admiration of a friend is not and can never be a replacement for the unconditional love of a parent.

In fact, I believe that this thinking, which is more prevalent than ever before, puts our children directly on the insecurity treadmill.

Hundreds of thousands of American parents, like the woman who offered me a ride, feel that their children's friendships stand in the way of a strong parent-child bond. Worse, they feel they can't compete—or *that they have no right to compete*—with their children's friends. They feel they have no right to demand precedence, and the kids in turn feel embarrassed to show any kind of dependency on their parents. Imagine this! We've come to a point where the people who bring a child into the world feel that they're imposing if they want a little time, and where showing love to the people who gave you life is cause for shame.

One episode of our show involved a father whose sixteen-year-old daughter had felt alienated from him since his divorce from her mother. We arranged a reconciliation, in which the father took responsibility for any hurt he may have caused his daughter. It was an extremely moving scene; many of the crew members found themselves getting emotional as this man asked his daughter's forgiveness for having neglected her during the long process of the divorce. The daughter began crying herself, and forgave him. But as he moved in to hug and kiss her, in this new spirit of closeness, his daughter pushed him away. It was one thing to cry, or to feel close to her father for his bravery in apologizing for his mistakes, quite another to get all mushy on camera—after all, she told me, her friends might watch the show!

Many children display a boundless appetite for spending time with people their own age—spending all day together at school, hanging out after school—but can barely tolerate spending ten minutes at the dinner table with their parents before rushing back to their friends on the phone and the computer. Their parents, who love and care for them, are treated as an annoyance. "Natalie, how did you do on that social studies test?" her mother asks. Natalie looks down at the table, as if the question came from her meat loaf rather than from a fellow human being. And then, with the pained look of a prisoner in the dock, she offers this lengthy soliloquy in response: "All right."

On weekends, one parent told me, it feels like she's running a hotel. The only time she sees her son is when he emerges from his room to collect snacks for the three teen-age boys who hide out in his room playing video games from Friday night until Sunday evening. She's considering offering a room-service menu—it's the only way she can think of to get into his room!

Now, I'm certainly not saying that friendship isn't important. Of course you want your child to be able to make and sustain real relationships outside of the family. Friendship, the idea that someone who is not related to you can become kin, is an amazing concept. Through our friends we see that we are all truly part of one family. Still, friendship is no substitute for *real* family. Indeed, I believe that when it comes to our children, we have corrupted the concept of friendship so that it has the potential to do more harm than good.

Therefore, when I say family first, I mean it. It is absolutely fatal to the family when friendships supplant the natural role of the parent.

Friends can entertain, but only parents can truly inspire.

When your children are closer to their friends than they are to you, the family is fundamentally decentralized and destabilized, with catastrophic consequences. You end up feeling used, the kids end up with little mature guidance, and the family is simply a collection of individuals who share a dormitory.

CONDITIONAL VS. UNCONDITIONAL LOVE

We have already discussed how badly children need the strength of character that comes from being loved unconditionally—knowing that they are cherished simply because they exist. The knowledge that you matter, no matter what, gives you a firm foundation from which your personality and character can develop in a healthy manner. But what happens when you swap that kind of love for the love you get from your friends?

The love you get from your friends is, by definition, conditional. Friends love you because you're funny, or because you're a good listener, or because you have a great sense of style. In other words, in friendship you are loved because of what you do rather than what you are. To be sure, the type of love that comes with friendship is important. Every one of us needs to feel that we're appreciated for our skills and talents, the things that set us apart. Indeed, this is why friendship is so important at a young age. Children need to feel validated by those to whom they are *not* related. They need to feel like they are special because they have gifts and blessings to bestow on others. There is a human need to feel special for what we can do, and not just what we are. But doing must always be subordinate to being.

But conditional love, by definition, lacks constancy, and conditional love is always limited by the condition itself. If you're appreciated for being a good listener, then the level of appreciation will depend directly on the level of the listening talent and the commitment you give to it. Having a bad week and want to complain yourself instead of listening to the latest installment in someone else's saga? Maybe your friends won't come around so much anymore.

Young people need a steadier and stronger diet, like a parent's love, which comes without provisions. From the core of our very being we love our kids, even if it's one-way—maybe even especially when it is! Often I will just look at my kids as they play or eat dinner. I stand in awe of what they mean to me, and how powerful a hold they exert. And this was true even when they were the tiniest of babies, which just goes to show how truly unconditional the love we feel for our children is. What, really, was that love based on when my daughter was three days old? Her scintillating conversation? Her stand-up routine? I laughed to hear the father of a newborn proclaim proudly: "Of course he recognizes me; he pees in my face every time I change him!" We love our kids, even before their eyes are fully open, with a ferocity that is unrivaled by any other human experience.

I call this unconditional love shown by parents to their children the nuclear love. In physics, there is the strong force and the weak force. The strong force, the nuclear force, is the force that keeps all the components of the atom together, the energy that serves as the very glue of earthly existence. This is the role that unconditional love plays in our children's lives; it is the force that holds together their fragile egos as they go through the considerable challenges of adolescence. It is at the heart of raising truly secure, happy children, and it is also the force that keeps a family together in the face of indescribable modern pressures.

We cannot afford to let an opposite attractor get in the way of this nuclear force as our children get older. Teenagers need friends, it's true. But it's the teenage years, more than any other stage in child development, that require parental involvement. Like any transition, adolescence involves self-doubt, loss of confidence, experimentation, confusion, and a colossal need for acceptance and reassurance. For years our society perversely worshipped teenage rage, but what has been almost blasphemy to admit is that what most teenagers desire is a firm hand to guide them through the transitional years and into adulthood. When teenagers don't get any of these things from their parents, they are left to get them from their peers—and we can all see how well that's going.

THE LIMITS OF CONDITIONAL LOVE

Nothing can replace the feeling you get from knowing that you're the center of someone's universe, and children can never get that feeling from anyone other than their parents.

I heard a story recently that perfectly illustrates this point. Birthdays are cause for a weeklong celebration in Daisy's family. Her grandparents usually fly in from Chicago for a series of small, meaningful rituals that they've observed since she was very little, like a trip to the Museum of Natural History followed by a special lunch at a restaurant nearby. Everything is capped off by a big birthday dinner, complete with a homemade pineapple upside-down cake (her favorite!) at the family home.

This year, her elderly grandparents didn't feel up to the trip, and fifteen-year-old Daisy asked her parents if she could spend her birthday night with her friends. Grudgingly, they agreed, and she was ecstatic—but it was a disappointing night. Daisy's friends were happy to celebrate with her, but they couldn't quite come up with the same level of enthusiasm she'd become accustomed to in years past. Instead of a long night spent at the center of everyone's attention, while her parents reminisced about how happy they were when she was born, how beautiful she'd been as a baby, and how proud they were of her now, her friends wished her a happy birthday, sang while she blew out the candles, and immediately returned to talking about which of the seniors was most likely to host a party that weekend.

Daisy learned, the hard way, that your friends can't make you feel like a princess the way your family can. To your friends, you're not royalty, you're just another really cool commoner.

EXPLORE YOUR INDIVIDUALITY

The unconditional love of a parent not only allows a child to revel in the center of all attention, but also allows them to grow and explore all the dimensions of their personality as well.

It is only within a family that a child can explore the full range of her individuality.

Friendship is based on mutual interests—we both like to play soccer, I like that band too! That is a wonderful thing; I truly value my friend Scott, who shares my love for debate and argues with me about everything. Although we're very different people, with different politics and opinions on important subjects, I don't have to misrepresent myself to be friends with him, because we're both adult, fully formed, and secure in our respective identities.

Adolescents don't yet have the inner character that makes them comfortable in their own skin. That's why peer pressure and conformity play such a huge role in growing up.

Kids tend naturally to want to fit in. I take pride in being a very involved father, but I have to confess that so many of my daughters' friends look alike that I can't always accurately tell them apart. They wear the same clothes (sometimes literally), they wear their hair the same way, they talk the same way, they like the same music. Think about it—isn't it true that teenagers stand out only as a group? The cool kids, the punk kids, the athletes—we brand them by their cliques because their identities are so fully subsumed into the herd.

I'm not criticizing teenagers. Lord knows, they suffer enough as they grow through that difficult stage without us adults dumping on them. But in their minds, they are conformists by necessity. Their relationships with their friends are based on mutuality, not individuality, and they sense, probably correctly, that these relationships are still too fragile to withstand a serious disagreement. To get along, you have to go along. But you can surely see how dangerous it is when these conditional, fair-weather relationships take center stage. You may not like the same clothes or music as your parents, but you can bet that they're not going to cut you dead and turn you into the subject of malicious gossip just because you like the wrong song or wear the wrong T-shirt. In your family, you're freer to explore your own opinions and tastes—an essential part of growing up—under the most benevolent of umbrellas, without the self-consciousness of worrying that you're doing or liking the wrong thing.

Indeed, I love the fact that each of my kids is different, and I encourage their differences. I love to point out what I consider to be each child's unique characteristic. I'll say,

"Mushki, you're special because you're the perfect, refined, feminine young lady. Chana, your uniqueness is a razor-sharp mind that unerringly finds the holes in anyone's argument. Shterny, you have the artistic temperament in the family. You always see a humorous and colorful dimension in every interaction that most others fail to notice. Mendy, you are the sponge of the family, forever soaking up—and remembering—every last thing that happens in this family, and a huge amount of trivia to boot. Shaina, you're the most determined one in the family. When you grow up, G-d willing, you'll be unstoppable because you're made of steel. Baba (Rochel Leah), you're special because you're full of sweetness and joy (and even if you weren't, you're special because you're my baby, baby girl). And Yosef, you're the rebel, the one who has consistently defeated your father's ability to control you. Man, you're a tiger.

WHO'S PARENTING THIS KID?

Kids today prefer friendship to family because friendship comes with no rules or real obligations; it's pure fun. Just look at the language kids use to describe spending time with their friends: there's "hanging out," which would seem more appropriate for clothing in a Laundromat than for two kids after school. Then there is "chilling," reminiscent of what a vodka bottle does in a freezer. "We're doing our own thing," they say—not the right thing, I notice.

It may seem trivial, but what all of these expressions have in common is a shared sense of abrogated responsibility. In effect, these expressions capture the very essence of adolescent friendship in modern-day America: carefree, irresponsible, immature, and bound to lead to something pretty empty.

When your kids spend too much time around their friends, the rigors of the home become intolerable to them. Of course they find their friends easier to be around; their friends don't hold them accountable for their poor grades in geometry, and they never tell them to clean up their rooms or what time they're expected home. But these expectations aren't a violation of a kid's civil rights, as you may have been made to feel.

It is your job as a parent to help your child grow up to be a meaningful member of society at large, and the rules you make and enforce are part of that.

I'm actually amazed at how many parents feel guilty about giving their children rules; it's one of the most common themes we find on *Shalom in the Home*. Many parents think they're violating some essential right of the child by making them do things they don't want to do. As host of the show, I want to show respect to all the courageous families I meet. But I also want to point out that you do children no favors by allowing them to exist in some kind of friend-chaperoned fantasyland, where nobody ever has to pick up after themselves or call when they're going to be late.

There's another reason to watch out for friendships that become too dominant: you and your kids will pay the price for more lax parenting elsewhere. I can't believe how easily we cede control of our most precious possessions! Did you really change all those diapers, disinfect every skinned knee, and supervise toothbrushing ten thousand times so that a more permissive parent could tell your daughter that it's okay to hang out with a guy in his bedroom with the door closed? I sure didn't, and that's something that's going to happen only over my dead body.

My own sister, who is a great and highly involved mom, saw her son practically fall apart at the seams when he fell under the influence of a bad group of friends. She discovered that he was smoking pot, and called the parents of the boy he got it from. Their reaction? They listened, but with the kind of impatience that is really saying, "Don't call us up and tell us our son is a bad kid." Their son then called my sister, and using the most vulgar profanity yelled at her for telling on him. Would you be happy knowing that these people—this foulmouthed friend and his blind parents—are determining what's okay and not okay for your child?

I also think that friendships, unless carefully managed, can be very hurtful to the other siblings in the house. When the family is together, siblings usually play (and sometimes fight) together. But when one sibling has a friend over, they often exclude the other family members. My daughters Chana and Mushki are only one year apart, so they've done everything together since they were children. But they are in separate grades at school, and have different friends as a result. One Sabbath, Mushki invited some of her friends over, and the group of them completely snubbed Chana, who was very upset (although in her pride she did not show any emotion at all).

I called Mushki aside and pointed out the consequences of her behavior: "You have to be the same person around your friends as you are when you're just with our family," I said. I later made it clear to all the kids that they are welcome to have friends stay with us for weekends, *but only if those friends are integrated into the family*. If the friends pull them away from the family, and I see them ignoring their siblings as a result, then I will put an end to friends on the weekend. Period. So now we have a rule that when friends are over, everyone who wants to participate may—no matter whose friends they are. This rule, far from oppressing our children, has led to some very important friendships across the rigid boundaries of age and grades. And it has led to many of those friends becoming a real part of our family, comfortable enough to pop by at any time.

I know that the pull of friendship can be difficult to counteract, and that some of these conversations can be very painful. I had just that kind of conversation with my daughter Chana last night. She is very bright, thank G-d, and is doing very well in school, the best student in our family, by far. She is also a brilliant writer. But she, always my most intense and passionate child, is not happy right now. We sat down together and I said, "You seem upset, and I think you're angry because you feel that I am too rigid about what you can and cannot do, and you're jealous of the freedom you saw your cousins had on our most recent trip to Miami. They can go out with boys, watch TV. They can spend hours on the phone if they wish. They're not pushed as hard as you are to do the right thing. And your oppression, if you want to call it that, is making you sad and angry and resentful of me."

We talked for a long time about my expectations of her, and about halfway through, I realized that I was, at my core, very wounded. I felt punished for being a responsible parent. I felt irritated that my daughter didn't understand that I'm the good guy in this situation, and that it's other parents, who are letting their kids squander their childhoods and waste their lives while all their potential stays locked up inside them, who need to change.

But after I overcame my own sense of victimhood, I came to a higher response: if my daughter feels that my parenting is a burden to her, then the only person I can blame is myself. I can't blame other parents, in comparison to whom I appear strict; I have to assume that I haven't been providing the inspiration that makes the healthier passions I promote seem as appealing as celebrity magazines and hanging out with boys.

Ultimately, I want her to understand that I am not circumscribing her freedom but protecting her from a false definition of the word. When your every fashion decision is based on the vulgar dictates of Madison Avenue, you're not really free. I want her to be free to find her own, independent identity, not one dictated by some designer or ad executive. And to make this live for her, to ignite the same passion in her that I feel on this subject, I will have to be more inspiring. I suspect that the conversation between us on this topic is not yet over, but I feel that we have laid the groundwork for further discussion together.

If you are one of the many parents who see that your children's friendships are compromising the strength and stability of your family, consider ways that you can prune back the overgrowth. Limit playdates and phone conversations, and assume the role of confidant and playmate yourself. Get out there and play with your kids. Make them laugh.

Tell them interesting stories. Share interesting facts with them. Stimulate their minds. Expand their emotions. Find ways to incorporate your children's friendships into your family life instead of always letting them take place outside of and away from it.

And model the appropriate role of friendship for your children by keeping your own friendships in harmony with your family life, so that your children don't feel they come second to your golf buddies. Just because you have adult guests at the table doesn't mean it has to be an adult night. Don't relegate your children to a separate table, or tell them to scamper off while you have the serious conversations, but involve them at every stage of the evening.

THE JOYS OF FRIENDSHIP
AND AN OPEN HOME

I hope that by illuminating these dangers I haven't given the impression that I believe all friendship is bad, and bad for our kids. In fact, I think the exact opposite.

One of the most important things we can do as parents is to provide a model of friendship and hospitality for our children.

I am always telling our children that as a Jewish family we must emulate the example of our patriarch Abraham, who was distinguished for his open tent and his hospitality. The canopy that Jewish couples get married under is a symbol of Abraham and Sarah's open tent. It is a roof with no walls, providing shelter but no barrier to entry. My wife and I try to emulate this example by opening our home and our hearts to a wide variety of people. We do this especially by inviting guests to our home for the Sabbath. Usually around twenty but sometimes as many as forty people join us for dinner, and we benefit from this blessing far more than our guests do. The conversation is fascinating, the home becomes interesting and stimulating, and my children learn a great deal by being exposed to so many different people, from all walks of life. This tradition has become as important to them as it is to me.

What is the difference between these types of friendships and the ones that decentralize the home? These relationships take place *within* the embrace of the family—they don't supplant it. Friendships should be like branches on a tree, growing out from the strong, sturdy trunk of the family, providing beauty and shelter and fruit without interfering with the structure of the tree itself. When children are anchored in their primary relationships with their siblings and their parents, then friendships are a wonderful gift. But if one branch becomes too heavy, it weakens the architecture of the entire structure, endangering the life of the tree.

ACTIVITY

CHAPTER SEVEN

The Parent as Camp Counselor

The best way to make children good is to make them happy.
—Oscar Wilde

At the tender age of fourteen, after five summers as a camper at sleepover camp, I became the junior counselor of my own bunk. They told me it would be a rewarding experience.

They lied.

I hated virtually every minute of it. The senior counselor was a lazy bum who slept most of the day, and I inadvertently found myself the proud father of ten eight-year-old brats. I spent hours a day cleaning up after them; one of them wet the bed every night, and that was my mess too. I worked sixteen-hour days, earning just enough per week to buy myself a six-pack of Coke. But, as miserable as the experience may have been, it taught me life's most valuable lesson about parenting—namely, that the best model of parenting is the parent as camp counselor.

While parents know many small things, the camp coun-selor knows one big thing: **In order to get kids to follow you, you have to inspire them and make it stimulating.**

And here is the interesting thing about camps: they're notorious for their rules. There's no sleeping in, and meals are mandatory. If you're not in bed by a certain time, the lights go out on you. Bunks are inspected for cleanliness, and if your underwear is on the floor, your whole bunk takes the demerit. Go near the lake without supervision and you're expelled.

Now, given all these rules, you'd think that kids would have to be dragged to camp kicking and screaming. But the exact opposite is true: kids love going to camp, and spend the whole year waiting to go back.

The answer lies with inspiration. The camp counselor understands that he cannot afford for any activity to seem boring or ordinary. If "lights out" is just time for bed, you're going to have a serious struggle getting ten boys to listen to a word you say, let alone into their bunks. But if "lights out" instead means the latest installment in the harrowing tale of swashbuckling adventure that you've been unfolding over the last week, they'll scramble into bed, anxious to hear what happens next. Good luck getting kids to play a soccer game if you sell it to them as "exercise." But watch what happens when you dangle the opportunity to best the arro-gant bunk next door; suddenly, you're going to see your kids play like Pele.

When I was a counselor, I remember gathering my bunk around me and explaining that we had the opportunity to take the lead in a camp-wide competition—but only if we did an extra-good job of cleaning our bunk for visiting day. I was tired of living in squalor, so I really sold it to them, giving them a speech worthy of a general addressing his troops before battle. I had gotten nowhere through threats and imprecations, so I tried inspiration and the power of persuasion instead, and it was like I had finally used the magic key. These kids took the beds out, scrubbed the floor by hand, removed every piece of clothing and refolded it, and made the sink and shower sparkle. The parents marveled: at home, the kids could barely be induced to make their beds, but when they were motivated, they went above and beyond the call of duty.

You can transform even the most mundane activities into something memorable and special—as long as you, like the camp counselor, understand that you're not a policeman but a source of inspiration.

It is essential for us to come up with—and participate in—wholesome and enjoyable activities for our children, just as their counselors do at camp.

This belief is one of the fundamental tenets of inspirational parenting, which is why Activity is the third branch of the PLANT parenting method. Our children need us to be actively involved in their lives, and we need to provide them with viable substitutes for the vapid, meaningless, and indeed often destructive activities foisted on them by popular culture and their friends.

The answer is for us to start thinking of ourselves as camp counselors, and our homes as bunks, and for us to fill family free time with activities that captivate and entertain all its members. We need to assume a more active role in our children's lives, motivating them with goals, exciting them about our values, and transmitting the things we are most passionate about. In this way, we can create a strong parent-child bond, and one that is based on vitality and exuberance.

BOREDOM IS THE ENEMY

The Talmud says that idleness breeds sinfulness, that when you have nothing to do you do what you ought not to do. Nobody knows this better than a parent—except a camp counselor.

When kids are bored, they inevitably do one of two things: they either disengage, zonking out in front of the boob tube, for example, or they misbehave, seeking fun and excitement by giving each other wedgies. Children are kinetic energy, energy that always seeks to be translated from the potential to the actual. They are like a cocked gun, or an arm bent back to throw a projectile. Of course, we don't want our children to lose that energy; it's what makes them so hungry, so curious, so endlessly interested in the world around them. That curiosity, which we'll discuss in greater detail in the next chapter, is the engine by which our children learn and grow. But we also don't want to see it lead them into the dark places. So we need to make sure that their profusion of energy is channeled into healthy pursuits.

Idleness is your child's greatest enemy, which makes it *your* greatest enemy. At camp, I quickly discovered that it was only when my kids were bored that they were itching to raid the bunk next door in the middle of the night to put shampoo in their hair and shave their eyebrows. If I told them great nighttime stories—and most of the time I scared the living daylights out of them as a form of sadistic payback—they lost all desire to fill the other campers' hair with toothpaste.

I learned to keep my bunk out of trouble by keeping them occupied. My philosophy was that if I channeled the kids' energy into engaging and edifying pursuits, I would not have to become a traffic cop that controlled his minions by giving out tickets. It worked. During the day I gave my campers sports activities and swimming, and at lunch and dinner they competed in history and trivia games at our table. There was never an idle moment, and although there were tons of iron-clad rules about bedtime and safety and cleaning up, I never heard anyone complain. And while the kids may not have been able to live without television or video games at home, there was none of that at camp, and nobody missed it. We were all tanned, fit, happy, and fully engaged by life. That dull glazed-over look that is common to so many kids was utterly absent at camp.

This is why we send our kids to camp, isn't it? We want them to interact with nature, and to breathe clean air. We want them to exercise just for the sheer fun of running down a hill or jumping off a dock, or the challenge of making an arrow hit the center of a target. We want them to unplug long enough to learn low-tech skills like woodworking and ceramics, singing and storytelling. We want them to learn what it means to live in a community, where you clean up your room because you share it with twelve other people, and nobody wants to see the socks you wore yesterday. And it works! We're astonished by how much our kids like it, and how well they behave. How obediently they stand in line for dinner! How immaculate the bunk is! How responsive they are to the words "lights out"!

Given how much our kids enjoy camp, not to mention how good it is for them, it seems logical that we can only gain from making our home life *more like camp* (and in my case, with eight kids, I really *do* have a camp). Successful counselors provide a high-octane day. Why should our homes be low-intensity by comparison?

BORED KIDS, BORING PARENTS

On one of the episodes of my parenting TV show, we interviewed the children of a family while the parents watched in a studio trailer outside. I asked the kids all kinds of questions about what was wrong with the home, what was missing in their relationships with their parents, and how things could be better. I consider myself to be a pretty spirited conversationalist, but getting answers from these kids was like pulling teeth. I had to struggle, using every conversational gambit at my disposal to get something—anything—even remotely coherent out of them. I felt that I would have had better luck interviewing dummies at Madame Tussaud's.

When I went out to the trailer to interview the parents about their children's responses, the mother exclaimed, "My kids looked like they were on drugs! They were utterly lifeless."

I'm not sure why she was surprised. Today, "leave me alone" is the refrain of American childhood. When I meet the teenagers who are going to be on our show, they can't wait to head back to their rooms so that they can watch TV, get online, or stick their earphones back in their heads. Everything around them—from the TV they watch to the malls they shop in, from the video games they play to the music they enjoy—is man-made and shallow. The real world bores them. They'd rather go to a film than to a mountain range; they'd rather be in a mosh pit at a concert than in a boat in an august sea; they'd rather IM each other about which celebrity has an eating disorder than have a conversation with their parents over dinner.

By now, you know my opinions about the pernicious effects of the celebrity-driven culture served up to our children by Hollywood and the record industry, with the result that much of what occupies our children is unwholesome. But that's not even the root of the problem; really, it's the activities themselves—or maybe I should say the *lack* thereof.

Our children spend their free time plugged in to various devices—and it's what they're *not* doing while they're plugged in that really concerns me. If they're passively watching TV or listening to music by themselves, they're not learning creative problem solving, they're not honing their social skills, they're not using their imaginations or developing logic, they're not building their growing muscles and hearts and lungs. And they're certainly not drawing any closer to their families.

Watching TV, surfing the Internet, shopping, playing video games—these activities are the very antithesis of childhood. They stunt children's natural creativity, expose them to adult themes that corrupt them, and make them indolent and lazy. I don't care if they're watching the most educational television program ever made—while they're watching it, they're not learning and growing by interacting with the world the way a child should.

So what is the answer? It cannot simply be to forbid these activities. Imposing restrictions without providing exciting alternatives to errant behavior is unfair, not to mention self-defeating. I remember my teacher and mentor, Rabbi Menachem Schneerson, the great Lubavitcher Rebbe, giving a public address in his synagogue to thousands of people. A child in the front was playing with a bunch of keys, to the distraction of the rebbe (and the rest of the congregation). The great man turned to the boy's father and said, "Let's find him something else to play with." Note, he did not say, "Take away those keys," and he didn't tell the child to stop playing. Instead, he encouraged the father to replace a disruptive activity with something more wholesome—but equally engaging.

We must do the same thing. If we take away television and the Internet, or severely limit them, then we have to supply something—and I believe something better—in their place. That means we will have to take a good hard look at ourselves and how we choose to spend *our* time, and it may require that we make some changes in the way we allocate our resources.

I fully realize that if I'm going to limit my children's time with friends because I don't want them pulled away from the family, then I better make the family pretty darn exciting. And that's what I try to do. At family dinnertime, we have history quizzes, debates about major news stories, prizes for the funniest joke. I'm always happy to share an interesting thing that happened to me that day, and I'll share in the most magnetic and charismatic way I can. I fully realize that it is not enough for me to simply tell my children stories; rather, I have to entertain them while I do it. Don't get me wrong. I mess up a lot and can often sink into my own world of worries, to the detriment of my kids. But I make the effort to stay engaged.

I have to confess: when I look at what goes on in many of the homes I visit, I'm not surprised that the kids are seeking excitement elsewhere, whether from their friends or the media. Their parents are boring! There's no inspiration there. Dad and Mom come home and slump down in front of the television, emerging every once in a while to yell about some infraction of the rules. Or they're so overwhelmed by work, home, and life in general that they're relieved that the kids keep to themselves, instead of fighting with each other or making demands on their parents.

It's not that these parents are intrinsically boring; rather, they have lost their own inspiration. They feel that they've had to abandon their own dreams, giving up on what they once wanted to be for a steady paycheck. Or that they have to sacrifice the things that really are important to them in order to succeed, because things like family time aren't appreciated in corporate America. They want to be decent, but they also want to be successful—and those things are all too often mutually exclusive in this society. Or they're trying to do both things as well as they possibly can, and they're exhausted. And if they're not inspired with their lives, how can they possibly hope to inspire their children?

The majority of Americans aren't inspired by their roles as parents, and they're not inspiring their kids.

But the idea that we're too tired to parent well assumes that we won't enjoy it—and when you parent inspirationally, the exact opposite is true. Has the workplace got you down? Then leave it behind when you come home, and reconnect with something much more nourishing. Antiseptic boss? Treat your wounds with the laughter of a child. Crushing deadlines? Spend a little while on a toddler's schedule, where it can take fifteen minutes to put toothpaste on a toothbrush.

It is our job as parents to provide a viable substitute for the activities that are destroying our children. It is our job to create an environment that is stimulating and fun—one that engages our children, the way they are meant to engage. If home is fun, then your kids won't be running off to their friends' homes or to the shopping mall. If your home is fun, then your kids won't need to constantly escape into the fantasy and mind-numbing world of TV. If *you* are fun, then your kids will want to be around you. And, just maybe, you'll have a little fun too.

DO IT *TOGETHER*

Some parents do recognize the importance of wholesome activity. My friend Shona's kids, for example, have an after-school schedule so complicated that it has to be coordinated on a massive whiteboard in their kitchen. Shona jokes that she's responsible for air traffic control as her kids rush from soccer practice to tae kwon do, from music lessons to art appreciation classes, from playdates with their friends to chess club.

Now, these activities might be more wholesome than surfing the Internet for celebrity gossip or cruising the mall, but I don't think they're the whole answer to the problem of America's youth. Finding healthy substitutes to engage our children, rather than leaving them to their own devices, is a key part of parenting, but it's not something that we can allow someone else to do.

We can't outsource our responsibilities to our kids; they need *us*.

Unfortunately, they're not getting us. We're too tired, too overextended, too broken, too busy chasing our own goals and dreams. We say that active parenting is too hard—it takes too much energy, too much effort. It's easier to stick them in front of a TV, or to let them run out to a friend's house.

Our kids feel this absence—and in my opinion, it is the number-one reason we're not raising worthy kids these days. Simply put, *we are not raising them*. They're raising themselves, with a little bit of overall guidance thrown in by us for good measure. Rather than being camp counselors, whose job it is to give our bunk constant, rewarding activities that produce healthy minds and hearts, we're school principals, handing down rules and meeting with our kids occasionally when problems come up.

After-school activities, in which someone *else* plays camp counselor to our kids and inspires them with some hobby or passion, are usurping our principal role as parents. Why are we surprised, then, when our kids talk to their ballet teachers instead of us, and cite their soccer coaches instead of their mothers and fathers as their heroes? Those are the people who are engaging them in activities with energy and enthusiasm, so naturally those are the people they feel connected to.

But that's a dangerous road to go down. Although other adults can and should play a role in our children's lives, *we* must be at the center of their lives. We have to be their heroes, their confidants, the member of the opposite sex who flatters them with our attention—because the connection that your child has to a coach or a teacher (and most certainly to his friends) isn't the kind of fundamental, permanent relationship that leads to securely rooted, confident children.

All of these external relationships are a thin substitute for the parental bond; no soccer coach is going to love your kid like you love him. Your child needs to be known by you—and how can you truly know him if you see him only for a couple of minutes a day? We, as parents, have to be at the center of our children's lives, and we can't do that if our only interactions with them take place for fifteen short minutes over cereal in the morning, or while we're ferrying them back and forth to their activities.

Experts also agree that it is very detrimental for kids to have these frenetic, overstuffed schedules. Of course this is true. When we expect our children to be out there, busy achieving, just the way we are, we neatly transmit the idea that they're valued for their accomplishments and their achievements—not simply for who they are. We're raising kids who are stressed out and stretched thin, just like their parents. And when we farm out our kids to all these different activities, we send another, even more dangerous message, one they will not hesitate to convey to their own children: all this "stuff" is more important than spending time with your family. That's why I believe that parents should be doing these activities themselves with their kids.

Of course, I do allow my kids to take some arts and sports classes, but I am careful to make sure that they don't interfere too much with time spent with the family. I have found that too often these after-school activities disrupt the evening for the whole family. Recently, for instance, my two youngest daughters lobbied very hard for gymnastics lessons. Since they do appear to have a talent in this area (and given that I can barely do a somersault), I signed them up for an eight-week session.

But, to tell the truth, I regretted my decision about three weeks into it. Because not only were my two little girls not home after school, but my wife, who was dropping them off, waiting for them, and picking them up, wasn't around either. So three important family members were missing in action during what I consider to be prime family time, and the whole family seemed lacking in cohesion as a result. When the three of them finally did come home at about seven thirty, the rest of the night was a rush: a quick dinner, homework, bedtime. There was no time for my girls to interact with their siblings, or for my wife to see the rest of the kids.

I finally called the girls to me and said, "I barely get to see you guys. Look, gymnastics may be important, but they're no substitute for family time. I don't need Olympic athletes in my family. I just need to see my little baby girls." They hadn't enjoyed the disruption any more than I had. They finished the alloted classes, but did not renew. Now, when they get home, they play with their two baby brothers outside rather than being absent from the family.

I recognize that I have the advantage of often being home when my kids arrive and therefore being able to do activities with them. If you can't always be home, then after-school activities would seem to make more sense. But even if you're not home, are your other kids there? Your kids will be able to hang out together, even in your absence, right? And if they're all being farmed out to various activities, how are they going to interact as siblings? I see so many homes where brothers and sisters only interact when they're fighting with each other. They need to play with each other as well.

Now, don't get me wrong. I recognize, of course, that there are kids with a natural talent for chess, music, or dance, and that talent should be given expression. I get it. But we parents so often think that our children's success will come from professional accomplishment, when in reality it will first and foremost come from emotional stability. And if they're raised in a home where they can play the violin but are desperately insecure because they're not getting enough love, then even their later professional achievements will sink into their inner abyss and never bring them happiness.

At most, I allow extracurricular activities once—at a stretch, twice—a week, and I insist that they're finished well before dinnertime. Most of the time, *I* am the after-school activity. And you should try to be it too. When my kids come home from school, we do something together—in the summertime, that's usually something outdoors, like swimming or bike riding or Rollerblading. In inclement weather, it could be sitting on the floor and reading books, or taking them to a bookstore, which I do about twice a month. It could be humorously imitating members of the family and getting the kids to laugh, which I usually do on the Sabbath. Whatever the activity is, I am the after-school camp counselor, not some karate instructor. It keeps me and my wife young and childlike, and it keeps our kids close to their parents.

In our family, playing is something we do *together*.

But I'm no tennis pro, you're thinking—or soccer guru, or chess grandmaster, or whatever the activity might be. One of the reasons I hear most from people who are outsourcing their responsibilities to their children (especially upper-middle-class people) is that they want them to have "the best"—and they know they're not it. But, as Marian Wright Edelman says, "Parents have become so convinced that educators know what is best for their children that they forget that they themselves are really the experts." You may not have a hundred-mile-an-hour fastball, but what you do have your kids need much more.

And yes, it does take a little work on your part. I know you're busy. We all are. You've spent all day working to support your family—now your family needs even more? But when I find myself supplying excuses for all the reasons I'm too tired to come up with something fun to do, I remind myself that there is always time for the things we think are truly important, and that there aren't that many things more important than being there for my kids.

It simply takes a little practice and effort. As is true for most people, my job doesn't fit neatly into the nine-to-five pigeonhole; there are always e-mails to answer, phone calls to return, and notes to make. But I so enjoy spending time with my kids that it's easy to put work on the back burner when I am with them. And I have no regrets about the business opportunities I might miss because I have dedicated this time to them. Unfortunately, the opposite is not true. When I was at Oxford, I ran a massive student organization consisting of thousands of students, and organized a world-class speaker program with at least two events per week. I hardly had time to breathe. I used to work most Sundays, while my kids and my wife went places and did activities without me.

To the rest of the world, I was a success, but I knew that I was not as happy and fulfilled as I could have been. And today, I think about those days not with a sense of victory, but with a feeling of failure. The very thought of working on Sundays and not spending them with my kids has become repulsive to me, and I look back at my workaholic self as an idiot, a man who squandered years of his youth at work when he could have been bike riding with his kids.

These days, I so look forward to every moment with my kids that I try my best to integrate them even into the professional responsibilities I have. For instance, every summer we take a trip in our RV, and last summer we went across the American South. Since I had to do my radio show daily, I had our RV outfitted as a mobile radio studio, and every day I broadcast a show from a different American city. It was great for my listeners, and it was great for my children. They learned a huge amount about America, its history, and its citizenry. And I brought the kids on the show a lot to discuss what they had seen. Every day was Take Your Daughter (or Son) to Work Day, and they not only learned a lot about America, but we learned a lot about one another.

And although they don't come with me while I'm filming *Shalom in the Home*, they are a very important part of it. I talk to them about every family I meet, and am fascinated to hear their insights and impressions of the problems I outline. They love meeting the families I counsel, and inviting those families to our home.

Like many parents, I do my share of worrying about work and money, but I see no reason to bring those worries home to interfere with my time with my kids—after all, that's what I go to work to do!

WHY SHOULD YOUR KIDS HAVE ALL THE FUN?

Too often, we see our kids as an imposition, but I strongly believe this is a problem of perception. Instead of seeing your camp counselorhood as a burden, I'd like to suggest that you embrace it and everything it brings with it.

Being with your children allows you to be the best version of yourself, a more lighthearted and fun version than the one who's barking orders over the phone to the office or frantically e-mailing a client. Being with your children puts you back in touch with your inner child and all the qualities we associate with childhood, including curiosity and joy.

I don't *want* to work all the time. And I am happy to use my children as my very good excuse to take a hike through the beauties of nature. When one of my kids expressed an interest in chess, I used it as an opportunity to brush up on my own rusty skills. There's a chess club at her school—but why should strangers get the time with her when we could have it together? I had forgotten how very much I enjoy the intellectual exercise and stillness that chess provides; what a pleasure it is to have such a good excuse to make time for it in my life.

I love going to the zoo and the aquarium; it's incredible that we have the opportunity to see animals that we would otherwise have to travel thousands of miles to see. I love to throw a football on a gorgeous fall day, and to jump into the big piles of leaves we've raked before putting them in garbage bags. I love to get my day's physical exercise, not by plugging away in bored agony on the treadmill but by Rollerblading with my kids or playing basketball or just chasing them around the yard. As far as I'm concerned, active parenting isn't a burden, it's a reward.

You may think that your children are standing in the way of your most authentic life. Is that really true? Or, as we will explore in the next chapter, is the act of transmitting your loves, passions, and values to the children you have brought into this world actually your most authentic life?

ACTIVITY

CHAPTER EIGHT

Passionate Parenting

Nothing you do for children is ever wasted. They seem not to
notice us, hovering, averting our eyes, and they seldom offer
thanks, but what we do for them is never wasted.

—Garrison Keillor

Doing activities with our children doesn't just consume
their excess energy. Acting as camp counselors gives us
the opportunity to truly parent—by which I mean to expose
our children to our passions, our most deeply held opinions
and thoughts, and our values. It gives us the chance to inspire them, the paramount job of a parent, and the principal
guarantor that we will continue to influence our children
even when we're not around.

In the book of Proverbs, King Solomon compares a parent to a bow and a child to an arrow; the bow continues to
shape the trajectory of the arrow long after the arrow has left
it. We speak of our children as our legacy. We scurry to make
sure that their college funds are in place, and that Aunt

Mathilda's heirloom silverware will be there for them when they get married. But isn't our real bequest to them something infinitely more precious: the values we have imparted to them over the course of their childhood that go on to flavor their entire lives?

There is a story in the Bible about Joseph resisting the wife of Potiphar when she tries to seduce him. Of course, it was extremely difficult for him to say no to her; he was a young man, at the height of his hormonal susceptibility, and she was very beautiful and very persuasive. How, then, did he manage to resist? The Talmud says that he saw an image of his father when he looked at her.

Even though they were separated by many miles, and although Joseph had not seen Jacob in many years, his father's pure values were still with him, guiding his behavior and making him strong. Joseph had been so close to his father, and so inspired by his father's example, that he permanently internalized his father's voice as his conscience.

Jacob was always with Joseph, and for me, that's the goal. I want the standards I have set to be the standards my kids try to live up to, even when we're far away from one another, and I hope that the values I have struggled to impart to them sustain my children long after I'm gone. I want to be permanently embedded in their heads, hearts, and souls, so that I help to shape and inspire their actions, whatever they do in life. After all, I *am* their father.

What better way to inspire your kids than to give them the gift of your own passions?

There is nothing more powerful than being in the presence of someone who is animated by something he feels strongly about. Certainly, the camp counselors who influenced me the most were those who had overt personal passions, and who did not hesitate to share them. For instance, I remember a counselor at camp in Montreal who loved nature and living the life of an outdoorsman. He had grown up in the urban streets, including a stint in one of the most violent gangs of the time, but he had turned his life around and become a religious Jew.

I used to watch him as he made a fire. As he kindled the wood, his own passion was kindled, and it sparkled in his eye. Often it would rain on these nights out, creating a miserable atmosphere, but he wouldn't succumb to the rain; instead, he stayed out there, keeping the fire going and telling us fascinating stories. He helped to create some of my most compelling memories from childhood, and I credit him in part with instilling in me a lifelong love of nature.

MY PASSIONS

My life is guided by five great passions, one for each finger on the hand. And it is with this hand, the hand of my passions, that I guide and inspire my children.

I have spent my life trying to choose and pursue hobbies and activities that are wholesome and uplifting, and it is now my great pleasure to share those things with my children. Although I encourage them to follow their own passions, I am also steadfast in trying to convey my own to them.

"Yawn," you're thinking. But this is where the activity component comes in. I don't communicate values to my children by delivering a lecture every night on the subject of "Shmuley's Passions." Instead, I take them Rollerblading on a warm Sunday afternoon, to a bookstore on a rainy one, or on a family RV trip. Remember, the point here is to inspire our children—to fire them up, get them excited about a wholesome life and enthusiastic about spending time with the family. You can't do any of that if nobody's having any fun.

I will share my passions with you in this section, as well as the ways I try to communicate these passions to my children. Even if yours are different, you will be able to see why this kind of activity is so important, both for you and for your kids, and how easily it is shared.

#1: G-d and Tradition

My first great passion is a love for G-d and tradition. I believe having solid roots and an understanding that your own life plays a role in a larger context is one of the most important elements in a happy and successful childhood. Indeed, this concept has such an important role in my way of thinking that it makes up an entire section of the PLANT parenting philosophy, which I will expand upon in a later chapter.

I have raised my children in an Orthodox Jewish home, and we keep all of the traditions that you associate with Orthodox Jews: we celebrate the Jewish holidays, keep a kosher home, and observe the Sabbath. But it is also very important to me that I explain to my children why we do these things, and why these things are so important to me personally. I believe that tradition is pivotal in every child's life, but ones carried out by rote are less effective than those that are followed out of a sense of inspiration and passion, and it is this that I hope to convey to my children.

#2: READING

My second passion is a love for reading and books.

I am a curious person, on an endless journey of constant discovery, which has enriched my life immeasurably. I used to read about a book a week, and while I struggle to find that kind of time now, reading remains one of my greatest passions.

It is my hope that giving my children a passion for books will fire their intellectual curiosity, one of the greatest virtues a child can cultivate, because it safeguards against the mother of all human enemies: boredom. Transcending the monotony of everyday life, the routine of everyday existence, is life's foremost challenge. And the gift of intellectual curiosity is the ability to find people, history, and life itself endlessly fascinating. I want my children to know that while they may not possess all the answers, they certainly do possess all the questions—and that there is a world of thinkers out there who have wrestled with many of the same ones, in ways that are endlessly interesting and illuminating.

I also hope that a true love of reading and knowledge for knowledge's sake will go some distance to counteract the very dangerous idea that learning and education are about impressing teachers, getting good grades, and getting into good colleges. When I was at Oxford, I was always saddened to see how few students read newspapers, or indeed, books outside of their coursework. They had been taught to master a subject rather than to engage life.

To express my love of reading and knowledge, I try to read to our kids—old and young!—every single night. I will often bring an interesting tidbit or factoid from a book that I'm reading to dinner as a conversation starter, and I love it even more when my kids bring one. And in addition to regularly taking my kids to bookstores and libraries, we also have "library at home," when we spread blankets in front of a fireplace and everyone reads a book for a few hours.

With the older kids what I usually read at night is a chapter of the Bible. It may sound like a really religious thing to do, but it's not. The Bible is the single most influential book of all time, filled with larger-than-life characters and breathtaking stories. As I write these lines, I have just finished reading the book of Samuel to my kids—one of history's most electrifying and instructive stories. They were riveted by the descriptions of David's bravery, and expressed strong opinions about Saul's incurable jealousy of David and the morality of David's actions in war.

My kids are always looking through my library and asking me lots of questions about the books I read, and I try to make sure they have access to books as a way to follow up on things they've shown an interest in. After we watched the movie *Titanic*, for instance, my kids were absolutely fascinated by the story. I went to the library and got two books on the tragedy that my children fought over and then devoured in a matter of hours.

A similar thing happened on our RV trip across the South. In Memphis, we visited Graceland, where I expounded on my theory that Elvis Presley was a classic example of the destructiveness of hubris. Here was a man whom G-d gave every talent, and yet he destroyed his life with drugs. The kids were mesmerized by this story of a man pulverized by success, and we stopped at the next exit to pick up a copy of Peter Guralnick's outstanding biography of Elvis, *Last Train to Memphis*. The four eldest children spent the duration of the trip taking turns with it.

Similarly, the kids were horrified and fascinated when we saw the balcony where Martin Luther King, Jr., was killed at the Lorraine Motel in that same city. Outside of King's hotel room is a marble slab with an inscription from the book of Genesis, originally applied to Joseph, that could not be more haunting or relevant: "And they said to each other, 'Behold, the dreamer cometh. Come let us slay him, and let us see what shall be with his dreams.' " I read the inscription to the kids with all the emotion I could muster, and it inspired them to go online and into my library to find out what they could about King, and the civil rights movement.

Even a subject as removed from our daily lives as Native American history came to life for my kids when we traveled through South Dakota and learned the history of the Lakota nation, with the larger-than-life figures of Sitting Bull and Red Cloud. There are any number of fascinating books on Little Big Horn, and I made sure that we got some so that my kids could feed their curiosity.

#3: History and Historical Sites

My third passion is a love for history and historical sites. I absolutely adore history. I love reading about history, watching historical documentaries, visiting historical sites, and feeling connected with the past.

Visiting a place like Pompeii, where I saw real Latin graffiti on the walls—two thousand years old!—was one of the most incredible experiences of my life. I love traveling through Israel and being surrounded by the holy places of the Bible and the ancient places of my people. When I lived in Europe, I always tried to find time to see all the great European historical sites. It really helped me in my efforts to understand the unique culture of a continent that has so influenced the rest of the world.

And as an American, I adore our country's history. I try to communicate my love of American history by making history come alive, and by incorporating it into our family vacations. When I give lectures in American cities, I will spend the morning of the lecture running around the city's environs to its historical places. Many times, my children are with me. And we dedicate our summers to traveling around America in an RV, with historical sites as our main stops. When I encounter evidence of the brilliance and bravery that led to the founding and triumphant survival of this country, I feel the glory of being an American.

I use any number of tools to make history come alive. For instance, last year I took my kids to the site of Washington's Crossing on the New Jersey–Pennsylvania border, where George Washington saved the faltering American Revolution with a bold nighttime surprise attack on the British in 1776. The children were mildly engaged as I showed them the point in the Delaware River where Washington and his ragged, frozen troops crossed. But they were completely spellbound by the audio version of David Hackett Fischer's *Washington's Crossing* that I played on the way home, with its mesmerizing account of the attack, the challenges Washington faced in mounting it, and how it turned the war around.

#4: NATURE AND THE OUTDOORS

My fourth passion is a love for nature and the great outdoors, and the belief that anything man can make G-d can make more beautifully.

We celebrate nature by going out into it! That might be walking, biking, or Rollerblading on the tree-lined roads around our house or in a nearby park. It might take the form of scuba diving, or skiing on one of America's majestic mountains, or hiking, as we do every summer.

This is a passion I share with my children not simply because I want them to understand that anything man can make, G-d can make more beautifully. I also want them to understand that they don't need to destroy nature to participate in it.

Too often, our response when we see something like a beautiful mountain range is one of conquest: "I want to conquer that mountain by climbing it." Or the impulse to turn it from G-d's creation into one of our own: "This would be a perfect place for a ski resort—we'll make a mint! We can put the lifts there, and the concession stand there. . . ." But neither of those are pure responses—they come from greed, from insecurity, from a desire for gain. I want my children instead to see something beautiful and marvel at it without feeling the need to put their mark on it. I want it to inspire them to marvel over all the creations on G-d's earth.

The opposite impulse is, quite frankly, destroying the landscape of this great country of ours. On one RV trip, we followed Lewis and Clark's trail through Montana. I told my kids that the highlight of the trip for me was going to be when we got to the Great Falls of the Missouri River, which were so powerful that Lewis and Clark had to give up the river, instead dragging all their stuff many miles by land. The children's anticipation built up with each stop, as we read from Stephen Ambrose's description of Lewis and Clark's travels.

But as we neared the Great Falls, we encountered the terrible stench of oil refineries, and when we arrived, we saw that a once-beautiful river had been destroyed by the ugliest dams and cement pilings. We took some pictures and left. But that night, as the kids all lay together in the RV— and there really is no better way to create family unity than a camping trip where everyone sleeps together in a tent or an RV—my kids expressed their horror at what had been done to such a beautiful, natural site. Even the stench was off-putting.

I tried to explain to them that the men who built all those dams and ruined the river weren't bad people, just adults who had utterly forgotten their childhoods. For them, the river was there to be used, not to create awe; people needed electricity, so they went and got it to produce electricity. "And now you see why," I said, "even kicking and screaming, I always drag you guys out into nature. It's not only that I want us to appreciate nature, but to appreciate the beauty of innocence."

#5: Immediate and Extended Family

On one of my mother's recent birthdays, I flew the whole family down to be with her. We had to do it as a surprise—not just because it added to the fun, but because I knew she'd be upset about the expense and effort we'd gone to. "It's just a birthday," I could hear her say. "Spend the money on the kids."

As we drove to the airport, here's what I said to them: "You know why we're flying down to Florida today? Not just because seeing you will make your grandmother happy, although it surely will. We're going down there as a way of showing our respect and admiration for her. We are like an honor guard, who stands at attention as a way of showing respect to a distinguished guest. This is a woman who worked two jobs to feed and clothe her five kids, yet she never turned anyone away from her table. In my eyes, she is a hero—like Thomas Jefferson or Madame Curie—and we're going to honor her."

It's important to me that my children respect my mother, because my fifth passion is a love for immediate and extended family. This book, of course, is about my love of immediate family. Beyond the nuclear family, it's important, of course, to have a close relationship with an extended network of family members. I mentioned this recently to a friend whose family has quite the opposite view. Her mother has not spoken to either of her brothers since the death of their mother ten years ago; her father hasn't spoken to his only sister in almost fifteen years. So my friend has absolutely no familial relationships with anyone except her immediate family. On one side, there are cousins she hasn't seen since she became an adult, and on the other there are cousins she has never even met.

"I never missed having those relationships," she told me. But I wonder—how can she possibly know? I believe that there is nothing quite like the relationships we have with our extended family members. It is, by definition, a unique type of relationship: they are separate from us, like friends are, but there is also a level of immediate intimacy that you can only have with your family.

My brothers and sisters are my best friends in the whole world. We grew up together, shared a home, shared the same parents, and shared the tragedy of their divorce. We know each other in a way that no one else will ever know us. It brings me great happiness to see our children together, and my children adore being with their cousins. Isn't it true that there are things we can only say to an aunt or uncle or grand-parent? My eldest sister is one of the only people who can get through fully to my daughter Chana when she is feeling down; they have a very close relationship.

I myself was blessed with a very close relationship with one of my father's brothers; we got to know each other very well during the three years I was in Yeshiva in Israel. One of the great luxuries about this relationship for me was how honest I could be about my own father; there is no disloyalty in talking honestly to someone who loves the person you're discussing as much as you do. So I was able to talk to my uncle about difficulties in my relationship with my father after my parents' divorce, and some things on their side of the family that had put strain on my own family, while he was able to show me a side of my father that I had not seen. And later, when he had troubles of his own, it was to me that he turned. He passed away a number of years ago, and we named our youngest child David in his memory.

The relationships we have with our extended family are filled with love, but there is none of the worry that we bring to our relationships with our own children; worrying is a parent's job. And it works the other way, too: my nephews can take advice from me that they would never be able to hear from their own fathers. They are like sons to me. Still, they are not my sons, and it is precisely because of this degree of separation that they can accept being mentored by me.

It is because these relationships are so unique and enjoyable that I put effort into making sure that my children know and have close relationships with their grandparents, their aunts and uncles, and their cousins. It's not hard to foster these relationships. We travel often to be with our extended family, and host them whenever they are close. We sometimes take vacations together, or go to one another's houses during school breaks (we're certainly not unhappy to flee New Jersey for Florida in the wintertime!). We try to spend as many holidays and festivals as we can together. And our children write and e-mail when they're apart.

I wonder: is my friend, who has all those cousins out there that she has never met, as complete a person as she would be if she was part of a more complex network? We'll never know, but I suspect not.

* * *

These five passions are the loves that have sustained me all my life. It is my great hope that even if my children find different things to love, they will get the same pleasure and sustenance from the things they care deeply about that I have gotten from mine.

WHAT ARE YOUR PASSIONS?

So ask yourself: what are your passions? Are there five things that interest you, and move you, and inspire you above all other things? And how can you translate them into activities that will not only convey their merits but provide you with a way to spend time with your children that all of you will enjoy?

For instance, I know a woman who is very concerned about ecology and the future of the planet. She also loves cooking and eating good food. So she and her young daughter go every Saturday morning to the farmer's market near their home and buy the seasonal produce, eggs, fish, and meat they find there.

They have relationships with the farmers, so that her daughter has learned respect for the earth and the people who work it to provide us with the food on our tables. Unlike most urban kids, she has a real understanding of where food comes from, instead of thinking that it magically appears in the supermarket. And when they go home, they make a delicious dinner together from what they have bought. In this way, they spend time together doing something both of them enjoy, and her daughter is gaining some very important skills—not just how to choose ripe vegetables and cook with them, but how to live a life that is passionate and responsible.

Another couple I know, inveterate world travelers, have taken their son with them on trips since he was an infant. They believe in exposing themselves to different experiences and different cultures, in part because of the way it enriches their understanding of their own home. Their son has "caught" their curiosity about the world, and learned a great deal of compassion from what he has seen.

I'm used to hearing parents scoff when I suggest more wholesome alternatives to the iPod/IM/video-game hegemony; I've had people laugh out loud at the thought of their sullen, too-cool-for-school teen on a family bike ride or listening to a story read aloud. But all bike rides aren't created equal—are you prepared to bring a camp counselor's energy and enthusiasm to yours?

If something is good, and interesting, and fun, our children will give it their attention.

And it is our mission, as parents, to make sure that the activities we promote are all of these things, so that spending time with the family is something to look forward to, not a chore to be dispatched or avoided.

And I think we do our children a disservice when we automatically discount these ideas as things they won't be interested in. One of the couples I worked with on our television show were amazed to report back to me that they'd overheard their fourteen-year-old son tell his friends he couldn't join them at a party on Saturday night because of the board-game night they'd instituted. "It's cool; the whole family is just hanging out. I'll catch you guys tomorrow."

Another family we worked with really flattered me when they came to a birthday party my wife threw for me and mentioned that they had taken up my passion for visiting historical sites with the kids. They had begun with Thomas Jefferson's plantation Monticello, designed (and redesigned) by Jefferson over a forty-year period, and were making their way to George Washington's home at Mount Vernon. They were surprised how easy it was to take these trips with their kids. Not only did they encounter less resistance than they thought they would, but their eldest son had begun reading Shelby Foote's magisterial history of the Civil War.

A former ballerina told me that she often takes her daughter, who loves the ballet, to watch professional rehearsals; she credits the tremendous hard work and discipline required to have been the major shaping force in her own character, and wants her daughter to appreciate how much sweat and practice goes into the beautiful, seemingly effortless dances she loves to watch.

Another friend bought his son a subscription to a jazz series; once a month, they go together to hear world-class musicians play the music they both love. In fact, I think that music merits a short digression here. If music is one of your passions, then it is one you should by all means explore with your children. There is a beat to the heart, and there are rhythms to life. And music, possessing both a rhythm and a beat, is the physical manifestation of our life force. Nothing captures our emotional state quite like music; it says what we cannot articulate in words. The fast-paced tunes of wedding music help revelers manifest their physical joy in dance.

A funeral dirge captures the solemn and heavy emptiness of our grief.

I am always grateful to music for what I consider to be its extraordinary generosity. When we hear music, it affects us physically, a gift that we pass along as we hum, clap, sway, and tap our feet. Movement is a spontaneous response to music, a natural impulse that swells up in the soul and releases itself in the flesh. And music is all-inclusive; it provides an outlet for those with great talent, but still manages to enrich the lives of those of us who have none. It has the strength to unite all the members of the human family and provide them with the inspiration necessary for a more joyous life. Indeed, if any element has the capacity to heal a fractured planet and bring pleasure to our lives, it is music.

Unfortunately, it is hard to celebrate modern music, and I watch what my children listen to as closely as I monitor what they watch on television, or what they do on the Internet. The trashy content and crude tunes make today's popular songs instantly forgettable. The focus has moved, so that music is now more of a visual medium than an aural one. Thinly talented performers rely on pyrotechnic displays or near nudity instead of their G-d-given vocal or instrumental talents to attract an audience.

So rather than letting my children listen to corrosive lyrics about people banging each other, or some other soul-deadening take on empty love, I try to choose music that will inspire them. As an Orthodox Jewish family, we listen primarily to Jewish music based on the verses of the book of King David's great hymn to G-d, the book of

Psalms. Of course, much of the great music of the last few centuries has been written to commemorate the glory of G-d, whether you're talking about Bach's *Passion*, Mahalia Jackson's rousing gospel songs, or Duke Ellington's Sacred Concerts.

When you love something, you can really make it sing for your children. And when you don't, you can't. For instance, I can be made to understand visual art on an intellectual level, but it is very rare that a painting or a sculpture moves my heart to sing the way a piece of music or the view of a mountain can. So although I do take my children to museums, and certainly encourage the ones who have an aptitude for seeing in this way, it is not an activity that we do as often as some others, because it is not something that particularly inspires me.

But I know a great many parents who have taken a child's interest or talents as a reason to become more knowledgeable and interested in something else. For instance, after her children loved the *Lord of the Rings* film trilogy, my friend Ginna decided to go back and read the original books by J.R.R. Tolkien. Why not read them out loud to her ten- and thirteen-year-old children? So now, all three of them curl up together in her bed and read together for forty-five minutes before bed, the way they used to when the children were little.

My friend Alison's daughter is hog-wild for animals, but they are not permitted to have pets in their building. So they volunteer on Saturday mornings at a veterinary clinic and shelter that specializes in rescued dogs and cats. Alison had never considered herself passionate about animals one way or the other, but her daughter's tremendous enthusiasm and compassion for all animals has really opened her eyes to the possibilities of these creatures. She says that she can feel her blood pressure go down as soon as she touches their soft fur, and acknowledges that a morning spent helping a completely vulnerable animal makes her feel considerably better about herself than one spent shopping or lazing around the house.

And, whether we are sharing our passions or exploring something that we hope will become a passion together, we cannot forget that it's our job to model the curiosity our kids should feel. My friend Jonathan dismissed my suggestion to use audiobooks in order to keep his daughters from their loud (and sometimes dangerous) squabbling in the backseat during the long commute to their school, but when their backseat DVD player broke, he tried it. He picked an abridged version of the classic novel *Madame Bovary*, which he had tried unsuccessfully to read a number of times in high school, finally resorting to the CliffsNotes to pass the exam. Everyone was a little bored at the beginning, but he stuck with it and encouraged them to do so, and eventually the story captured their imaginations. Jonathan's kids still watch more TV than he would like, but the whole family went to the library together to choose their next audiobook, and he can't complain about the tranquil backseat and their rapt attention to what is developing between Mr. Darcy and Elizabeth Bennet on the way to school these days.

NO SHORTCUTS

It has taken some doing for me to rearrange my life in order to have this time to spend with my children, and there are certainly days when it is hard for me to muster the enthusiasm and energy that I need to play camp counselor. But our family is so much stronger as a result that it's easy to remember why I don't take shortcuts.

That's not to say I'm not sometimes tempted. I do recognize that choosing to create wholesome activity isn't always the easiest route. My family is a camping family, and we own an RV that we take on long road trips. Sometimes the kids can be in the RV for up to ten hours at a time; I don't need to tell you how trying that can be. Now, it would be very easy for me to put an endless series of mindless DVDs on the TV for my kids to watch, so that they'd stay out of each other's hair, and mine. And to be honest, I sometimes give in and let them watch some inane movie. But we have the RV so that we can experience America together as a family, not so we can soak up stupid culture at sixty-five miles an hour.

So the challenge falls to me and my wife to make the time interesting and inspiring for all of us. We play board games with the kids; they do a lot of art. I lob trivia questions at them and share historical factoids. We especially love playing geography. We listen to nonfiction on tape, often stories that relate to the sites we've visited.

I know that my children have benefited from this time spent together. First of all, they know that my wife and I have chosen to spend time with them, which proves the unconditional nature of our love. Children learn best by example, by the behavior that you model. If you come home from work at a decent hour and read to them from good books, they are going to feel that those are the sorts of things that are important. But if you prioritize buying them clothes and toys, they will soon enough pick up the message that it's material possessions that count above all in life. That's why this chapter isn't about passion, but about activity.

I also feel that we know each other better than most families do! Remember the days when you knew every single thing there was to know about your son or daughter? You knew that the blue bunny was good for naps, but only the pink elephant would do at bedtime; you knew that she preferred her grilled cheese sandwiches cut in triangles, while the peanut butter ones tasted better cut in squares. Spending this kind of quality time together may not give you back that level of intimacy, but I bet you will be very pleasantly surprised by the insights your children can bring to the things you feel strongly about, and how much insight you gain into their rapidly developing characters as a result.

And that flow of information goes both ways. By sharing my passions, I help my children understand why I think the way I do, and care about the things I care about. Knowing what I stand for helps them to "get" me. That, in turn, helps them to understand why we live the way we do, and have the rules we have. I'm not just a dictator to them, an unknowable force who wantonly forbids movies and dating and other things of which I don't approve. Instead, I'm a person who cares passionately about a wide variety of things—not least of which is making sure that my children have a wonderful and edifying childhood.

NOVELTY

CHAPTER NINE

Finding the Wonder in the Everyday

Behold the child, by nature's kindly law,
pleased with a rattle, tickled with a straw.
—Alexander Pope

You go to Target to buy laundry detergent and toilet paper; your kids, of course, end up in the toy aisle, whining for an Elmo that dances. They already have an Elmo that wiggles and one that sings, but you give in and buy the new one anyway. Predictably, within the week, new Elmo is landfill, sharing space with all the other broken, unloved toys your children "couldn't live without" when they begged you for them. A waste of space and money, but there's no real harm done, right?

I'm not so sure. Isn't something infinitely precious lost when we lose our sense of wonder? Isn't there something inherently tragic about an inability to find something interesting in what you already have? Isn't the ability to see the magical quality in even the most mundane event or object one of the great gifts of childhood?

Our children are born with a tremendous natural curiosity. When we attempt to satiate that curiosity with plastic junk and garbage TV, we open the door to a multitude of evils. Soon, it's no longer an Elmo that they're discarding but a wife or a job, because these things eventually bore them too. What, after all, is the defining characteristic of the unhappy American, if not this quality of being permanently dissatisfied? We job-hop, house-hop, and marriage-hop, desperately seeking happiness in upgrades, replacing our most valuable treasures with newer, souped-up models. But is our job really boring, or have we merely lost the ability to take pride and satisfaction from good work well done? Has your wife really grown less beautiful as she has aged, or have you simply gotten more cynical, so that you can no longer see how beautiful she is and desire something younger and augmented instead?

I know that much of this boredom in later life can be prevented if children are encouraged to hold on to their natural sense of wonder, their talent for making the everyday ever new.

I sometimes think that the principal work of parenting is to move our children *away* from unhealthy attractions and *toward* healthy ones. Let's face it: nobody has to entice their children to play video games, but we do have to work hard to get them to do their homework, eat their Brussels sprouts, and say please and thank you. We do this so they will develop good habits and a worldview that will allow them to find true happiness and health throughout the rest of their lives, in the way that a child who has grown up thinking of fruit as a snack will continue to choose healthy foods as she grows. The more difficult the journey, the more fulfilling the reward.

In this vein, I believe there is no more important lesson that we can possibly impart to our children than preserving the ability to see everything—no matter how routine—as if for the first time. And in so doing, perhaps we too can recover some of this ability within ourselves, so that we can also see the miracles in the everyday.

TAPPING INTO THE NATURAL CURIOSITY OF A CHILD

We all know that children are naturally curious, organically attracted by the new and different. They have to be—it's how they learn. But this innate curiosity is really an amazing gift, and one that has the potential to enrich everyone who spends time with them.

One of the problems of growing older is how the special becomes ordinary, the magical becomes predictable, and the miraculous becomes routine. We get desensitized, cynical, and bored. Look, if you will, at your marriage as an example. When you first started dating, you were endlessly interested in the other person; you wanted to know everything about him: how he grew up, what his relationship with his parents was like, his professional goals. You wanted to know about the people he had worked with, the places he traveled to, and his favorite movies. And you were electrified by even the simplest touch.

But as time went on, you may have found that you settled into a predictable routine. If your marriage is a good one, you probably love your husband much more deeply than you did when you first started dating, but the novelty—and therefore, much of the excitement—has worn off. You don't wait for him to come home from work the way you used to wait for him to pick you up for a date. You've lost your sense of wonder about him, so that what used to be earth-shattering has now become routine.

Unfortunately, this sense of "been there, done that" is what undermines most marriages. When novelty is lost, life gets boring, and when life gets boring, we learn to disengage, retreating more and more into fantasy worlds, where we can find the novelty we crave. So, to continue the marital example, we spend date night at the movies instead of in conversation, or dip into pornography, or have affairs with the neighbors, whose secrets we don't yet know.

You cannot remain engaged by life if you don't maintain a sense of wonder.

For most of us, the problem is in our perception: life is really a collection of outstanding and inspiring events. When you can see the miracles in nature and the unique aspect to even the most banal thing, you are bound to be fully absorbed in and engaged by your life. Truly happy people know how to take the ordinary things and make them extraordinary. As one man I counseled said, "My wife is so endlessly interesting to me, she's endlessly erotic; it's like taking a new woman to bed every night."

Now, the sense of wonder I am describing comes naturally to a child. Young children find routines comforting, not cloying. Although the sequence is always the same—dinner, bath time, stories—the cycle is ever-renewing for them.

There's always something new to taste, and a new flotation experiment to conduct. There's always pleasure to be found in cuddling up to someone who cares about you, and comfort in the simple, repetitive rhythms of *Goodnight Moon*. By contrast, an adult thinks, "My life is stifling me: every day I get up, kiss the same woman good-bye, drive the same road to the same job. Is this as good as it gets? Is this what I had planned for my life? I'm so depressed I could kill myself!"

It doesn't take a lot to impress a child. A simple hug, a story read with gusto, an anthill will do. But for *us* it won't do, and they quickly learn from our insatiability. Pretty soon they become insufferable, the spoiled brats we complain about, for whom nothing is good enough. And we wonder why we were punished with these satanic kids, when really, we created them.

Too often, *we* snuff out our children's sense of wonder.

A child wakes up after an overnight snowfall and sees her ordinary world reinvented, gift wrapped in beauty and draped in mysterious silence. It's magic for her—and maybe, for a moment, for us too. But the child is all too soon pulled into the adult world of cynicism, practicality, and complaint, so that she becomes blinded to the beauty of an icicle in the sunlight by the prospects of a sidewalk to salt, traffic snarls, and the ugly gray slush to come.

One of the problems is how materialistic our society has become. This has led to the establishment of an unfortunate cash nexus between parents and children, whereby it is widely believed that gifts can act as a substitute for love. The old joke goes, "My daughter used to see me as a dreamboat. Now she sees me as a supply ship." Don't we invite that, when we act as pay stations, leaving PlayStations to raise our kids?

One family we had on our TV show had a young son, nine years old, who was a terror—truly spoiled rotten. Nothing was good enough for him, and he yelled at his parents constantly to get what he wanted, and appreciated none of it when it came. His parents wanted to know how they had raised such a monster—and to show them, all we had to do was splice together some video of how they spoke to one another. Dad comes home, sees what's for dinner, snipes about how they had the exact same dish two nights ago, and conspicuously orders something in from a restaurant. He spends the rest of the night complaining about how much he hates his job, how much he hates his boss, and how he wants to replace his two-year-old car. His wife, meanwhile, complains constantly about how bored she is: they never go anywhere or do anything, she says.

Maybe their life is boring, but their own insatiability is clearly where their son's demons are coming from. I told them, "The problem with your child is he *isn't* a child. You have raised a tiny, cynical adult." The father said, "That's exactly right! I'm amazed that you were able to diagnose that accurately," as if any neutral observer could not have seen the problem immediately. But the problem he failed to see was the real one: that he had lost those childlike qualities as well.

The only kind of parent that can really inspire his children with novelty and wonder is a parent who has a very good relationship with his own inner child. In order to help our children hold on to this precious quality, we too must be in touch with our own innate ability to be moved by the everyday.

And, rest assured, even if you feel that you have gotten very far away from the kind of person who sees a winter wonderland instead of the backache that will come from shoveling the drive, all is not lost. Because I think we can greatly benefit from exposing our jaded adult selves to the open innocence of our children. Our children have a tremendous gift to give us, if only we are receptive to it. We must open our own hearts to wonderment, and the many everyday miracles that surround us: a sunset, or the complex machine that is the human hand.

Certainly, for me, this reexploration of novelty is one of the great treasures of parenthood.

Our children reintroduce us to the majesty of the everyday and the magic of the seemingly mundane.

First of all, our children are themselves novel, every single day. They literally change and grow right before our very eyes. It seems that every time you turn around, they've learned another word, grown another inch, or come up with a new knock-knock joke.

And our love for them is ever-renewing; it never diminishes, but grows and grows with time. We take pictures of our children as if they were celebrities, and while the same routines unfold over and over again, we find new enjoyment in seeing the baby taste strawberries, or watching a teenager do a layup. Before you were a parent, could you possibly have imagined how enthralled you'd be just to hear someone say "bye-bye"?

Simply being around our children restores our innocence and renews our appreciation for the little things—an appreciation that we may have lost. Indeed, spending time with a very young child can be an education in making the everyday new, if you have the patience and wisdom to follow their lead. They can spend hours on their stomachs, staring at the differences between blades of grass, and watching the ants carry tiny bits of food to and from their holes. Where is it written that parents do all the teaching? I like to get down on my belly with them, so that I can try to see and learn from what they're seeing.

"G-d is in the details," the famous architect said—and nobody knows that better than a child. This week, I watched a two-year-old study a small model taxi for almost twenty minutes. He looked at the minutely painted checkerboard design on its side, the way the tiny wheels spun, the miniscule hinges that allowed the small door to open, and the molded plastic steering wheel inside. He held it upside down to see if the wheels would still turn, and held it up to his ear so that he could more closely hear the noise when they did. Just watching him made me more attentive to the details for the rest of the day, made me more curious about how something like the coffeemaker worked, and more grateful that it does.

How tragic it is to trade your curiosity about (and satisfaction in) the tiny world of an ant or a miniature car for the shallow pleasures marketed to our children by Hollywood and the video game industry! Preserving our children's natural sense of awe and wonder is one of our most important roles as parents; we must help our kids hang on to how impressed they are with the simplest things. We dare not allow our corruption to corrupt them. Because, for all its tremendous benefits, curiosity is also behind an enormous amount of the world's unhappiness, and we must help our children to navigate around its pitfalls.

THE DARK SIDE OF CURIOSITY

Curiosity may power a sense of wonder, and it may be how you learn, but it is also how you get cast out of the Garden of Eden—by focusing on the one fruit you haven't yet tasted. It is this "dark side" of curiosity that we have to be mindful of.

It can be tempting to placate our children's appetite for the new with confections—the empty calories of popular music, disposable toys, and the latest clothes. But, as you probably know, vulgar, manipulative entertainments won't satisfy them for long. They'll always need more, like the serpent, cursed by G-d to slither on his belly and to eat dust. Dust, like junk culture, is everywhere, but it's fundamentally unsatisfying. You can eat and eat and eat, and you'll never have enough—the same way that you will never be satisfied, at any real level, no matter how many hours of mindless television you log, no matter how many pornographic images you view on the Internet, no matter how many new shoes you buy.

An inner emptiness is the motor force of insatiability.

Adam and Eve were infected by this toxic, adult insatiability; it poisoned their childlike innocence. Now, our children face the same threat. We must act, so that they don't need to become addicted to frills in order to sustain their interest in life.

We don't have to look too closely to see how our failure to renew our children's sense of awe, novelty, and wonder is ruining our kids. They're like junk-food addicts, tasting everything in the culture that is shallow, unwholesome, and impure. And the more they eat it, the more they need it. New novelists can't get published and many of the classics are out of print, but every week there's a new celebrity magazine franchise on the shelves—they can't keep up with the demand! So instead of being inspired by someone's imagination or one of the great books, our children are fueled with stories about which overpaid actor has gotten another overpaid actor pregnant before leaving the overpaid actor he was married to. Rather than look up to Mom and Dad as heroes, they look up to sports figures and rappers as their heroes, even if these figures lead deeply immoral lives. Of course they're unsatisfied! There's nothing remotely nourishing or sustaining about these confections.

I want my children to be able to take pleasure in the everyday, so that they can avoid the trap of insatiability that snares so many of us. I want them to love the home they have, no matter what size it is. I want them to love the person they marry as much on their twentieth anniversary as they do in the first year. I want them to enjoy their jobs, so that they don't constantly have to escape to fake adventures. And the only way I know to give them that ability to sustain themselves as adults is not to allow them to trade their sense of wonder for something cheaper as children.

Novelty

Chapter Ten

Making the Ordinary Extraordinary

If a child is to keep alive his inborn sense of wonder,
he needs the companionship of at least one adult who can share it,
rediscovering with him the joy, excitement and
mystery of the world we live in.
—Rachel Carson

Through inspirational parenting, we can nurture our children's natural sense of wonder and awe, satisfying their curiosity with that which is wholesome, not transient. In so doing, we can remind ourselves to appreciate the glorious blessings we already enjoy.

As we will see in this chapter, there are a great many simple things we can do to help our children hold on to their innate sense of curiosity. We can start by saying no to so many of the disposable pleasures that threaten to inundate them. We can make sure not to let our own boredom or irritation show, instead encouraging their endless questions and demonstrating an interest in and appreciation for life's everyday miracles.

But at another level, we must show them that life's real treasures come when they delve *deeper*. They have two choices in life: they can seek horizontal renewal and novelty, by chasing endless, unsatisfying versions of the same thing; or they can truly plumb the depths of what they already have, by getting to know everything there is to know about someone or something, finding endless ways to appreciate and understand them—and therefore endless fascination.

Learning to renew ourselves *vertically*, finding something deeper in what we already have, is the essence of a fulfilling life.

This is not just a way to get off the Elmo-go-round of discarded toys, it is a tool, a skill set that you are giving your children, one that will last them a lifetime. And, as with all the tenets of inspirational parenting, helping our children to preserve this essential quality has the potential to greatly expand our own worlds, as well: seize the opportunity to recapture your own sense of wonder, even as you encourage your children to hang on to their own.

Let us explore some strategies in more depth.

#1: SAY NO—AND GIVE THEM SOMETHING BETTER

The first thing we can do to help our children maintain their sense of wonder—and it is something I see precious few parents having the courage to do—is to say no.

Here, we return to the concept of protection, the idea that a parent is first and foremost a guardian, above and beyond all other roles.

Maintaining your child's innocence and sense of

wonder will sometimes mean that you have to say no to indulging the dark side of your child's curiosity.

We do that by putting Elmo back on the shelf.

It's very easy to capitulate to our children's boredom. If a new toy, a teen magazine, or a new shirt will stop them from whining and make them happy, why not give it to them? I'm not saying that your children should have nothing that they want; please trust me, it's not like my children sit in empty rooms wearing rags. And I'm not even opposed to the occasional treat; as I said to my daughter Chana when buying her some bangles in Mexico City, "Thirty dollars to see my baby girl smile is one terrific bargain."

But when we establish relentless, needless consumption as a pattern, we're not indulging our children so much as we are stealing from them. We are stealing their confidence in their ability to entertain themselves with what they already have, forcing them to turn outside of themselves in search of something to answer their hungers. This is why we don't indulge in much of the rampant commercialism that characterizes so many American homes. I find so much of American culture vulgar and stupid, and refuse to allow them to get hooked by the latest silly fad, as if they are (and I am) nothing but some puppet manipulated and controlled by advertisers. As parents, it's our job to say, "It's enough." "No, you are not getting a new bicycle; there's absolutely nothing wrong with the one you have." "No, you're not buying the new iPod. Just delete some of the songs on your old one, and you'll have room to fit all the songs you need to hear." Not that I'm all that crazy about kids having their own iPods in the first place.

It's not enough to talk the talk—you have to walk the walk.

Too often, we fall back on vacations and family outings as a way to distract our kids. But when we do this, we actually feed our children's boredom—in a sense, we're conceding the point that there is nothing of value to be found in the things that already surround us. Some of my kids came home early the other day; their uncle was visiting, and they wanted to take him to a restaurant, although we'd all gone out the night before. I have to admit, I was tempted. I was myself tired from a hectic day, and looking for something to distract myself. But I recognized the impulse we were all having, and quenched it. "Why," I asked them, "isn't simply having him here enough? We'll have dinner in the kitchen together. Afterward, we can all sit in the living room and ask him questions, tell him about our RV trip last weekend, and show him the pictures we took. Let's share our everyday life with him, and let that experience make our lives new again."

This is not to say that I'm against family outings and vacations—quite the contrary! But we need to make sure that what we choose to *do* reinforces what we say. Passive activities, like taking your children to the movies, don't reinforce all the values we've been talking about. And don't cop out by choosing artificial activities; we do our children a terrible disservice when we show them that the artificial and contrived are more impressive to us than the natural and the real. If you only take your kids for vacations to Disney World or amusement parks, you're essentially telling them that concrete and contrived twists on roller coasters are what makes your heart beat faster. Is that really the message you want to send?

I am vocally opposed to the tradition of taking kids to the shopping mall as a form of family outing. The malls, of course, have responded to this trend by making themselves into little hermetically sealed environments, where you can spend hours—days!—going from junk food to junk movies to junk clothing, without ever seeing the light of the sun. But it's a mistake to fall into this trap. If you take your family to the shopping mall on a Sunday afternoon, you're showing them that novelty comes through acquisition. In this way, we show our kids that we too are empty vessels, black holes, so bored with life that we need to stuff ourselves with flimsy material objects just to feel fulfilled. If you need something, okay—go out and buy it. But if you don't, then what in G-d's name are you doing at a mall? Trying to create a need, just because you're bored? This is what you want to teach your children?

Try going on a hike instead. I know—you may have to use a cattle prod to get them into the car to go for that hike, but I bet it will be worth it, if not the first time, then the third. Because you know what? Nature really is cool. It really *is* wondrous. And with repeated exposures—the very same way, incidentally, that they became shopaholics—they will become sensitized to the awe and beauty of nature. I promise: keep trying, and they'll stop rolling their eyes, and open them instead. You'll witness a miraculous transformation. Because inside the fierce exterior of that sullen kid is a child who is still bursting with curiosity and a sense of wonder, and just needs a little help to get back in touch with those sensations.

#2: ENCOURAGE THEIR NATURAL CURIOSITY

Another way you can make everything appear new to your children is simply by encouraging their natural curiosity.

Now, I have eight children, thank G-d, so I know well how exasperating it can be when they go through the (seemingly never-ending) "tell me why" phase. Why is the sky blue? Why is grass green? Why can't our car fly? Why is it sunny? Why do you have a beard? Why doesn't Mommy have a beard? Why can't I have a beard? Why? Why? Why not?

What helps me to be patient is remembering that curiosity is a gift—a measure of the joy you feel about life and how it works. We have to be super careful never to snuff out our children's natural sense of curiosity; if you treat your children's questions like they're a nuisance, you can be sure they will stop asking them. So I happily answer whatever my children throw at me. And it can be very interesting, for all of us, when I allow myself to be directed down the path of their research. For instance, I didn't know what kind of sounds zebras make until my youngest son asked me and I asked Google. (It's an odd squeak, actually.) It had never occurred to me to ask. Best of all, our investigation led us to the unsettling laugh of a hyena, a perfectly terrifying bear growl, and the majestic roar of a lion.

How do you respond when your young children point out something they think is interesting? Do you make an attempt to see it from their perspective, or do you blow them off with a thoughtless "That's nice, dear"? Do you look them in the eye when they ask you a question, or do you pretend to listen when really your mind is someplace else? It's essential to always show how impressed you are with everything your child brings to your attention, from seashells to worms, from loose teeth to report cards.

Don't forget that your children watch as you move

through the world, and they model themselves on your behavior. If you seem interested, they'll be interested. But if you moan and groan, finding endless fault with everything that surrounds you, they will too.

#3: APPRECIATE THE EVERYDAY YOURSELF

When your child brings you a seashell, don't just *act* like you're appreciating it—appreciate it! By doing so, you are modeling curiosity, teaching your children to see everything as new by seeing it that way yourself. In order to do this, you may have to change the way you see and react to the world around you—and that's a good thing. Are you really so jaded that you can't look at the complicated whorls and varied colors of a seashell without seeing the beauty and mystery in it?

We take the same walk to our synagogue every single Saturday. Every week, I make it a point to notice and point out one thing we haven't seen before, whether it's a patch of wildflowers by the side of the road or an architectural detail on one of the houses we pass. When we sit down to dinner together, as we do almost every night, I draw their attention to how lucky I feel to be there with them. I try to compliment my wife on the meal, even if it's a recipe we've eaten thousands of times before. And although I do this primarily to hone my children's sense of wonder, it is a very useful thing for me to be reminded of how beautiful my surroundings are, and I find that my wife's delicious Bolognese sauce always tastes better when I take a moment to appreciate it.

I have worked hard to always maintain my natural curiosity about people, and the work I do has only honed it. So when I meet people, I want to know about them, about their families, their relationships with their spouses and children, what they think about the headlines on the front page and the state of our culture. I suspect this is part of the reason that my children are so confident and composed around adults, and why they ask as many questions of our guests as they answer.

Please don't think that I'm tooting my own horn here. I try to make an effort because *I too want a life of wonder.* I too want a life fueled by interest and curiosity, so that I don't have to escape boredom by watching something new on TV or buying myself something at the mall. I want to live, not just exist; I want to climb the mountain too.

#4: GIVE YOUR CHILDREN THE EXPERIENCES THAT WILL GIVE THEM PERSPECTIVE

As I previously mentioned, I love learning about history. And one of the very important reasons I find it so endlessly fascinating is because of the perspective it affords me.

It's easy, as an American, to take our tremendous freedoms for granted as we get up, go to work, come home, eat dinner, and go to bed. But when I stand at the Lincoln Memorial, I come face-to-face with the legacy of a simple man who grew up in poverty to become one of the greatest human beings this country has ever produced. His willingness to confront slavery, the great evil of American history, was the result not of great wealth or power but of moral courage and the ability to see the divine image in every human being.

That's inspiration. And when I stand at the dark granite slab of the Vietnam War Memorial, I am reminded that the liberty I can take for granted every single day has been continually purchased by the blood of ordinary people, people just like me, who made themselves extraordinary by their willingness to sacrifice themselves for others.

This is one of the reasons I like to take my children to historical sites. It's very easy, even at their tender age, for them to become jaded, but history can be a powerful wake-up call. For instance, it was a revelation for them to see Little Rock Central High School in Arkansas, where in 1957 nine black students challenged segregated education simply by going to school. It looks like an ordinary public school from the outside, so I had to make it live for my children: "You complain about your teachers, about the food in the cafeteria, about how much homework you have," I said. "But just imagine what it would be like if you had to struggle in the morning through a riotous mob, with people—adults!—throwing things at you and screaming filthy, hateful epithets, just to get to that teacher you complain about. Imagine that you had risked beatings—indeed, your very life!—to get those homework assignments you resent so much."

Of course, they had heard the story already, but standing at the site and imagining themselves in those nine students' shoes made that story—and the lesson I had hoped to impart to them—come alive. At Little Rock, school—plain old school—became new for my children again.

And as we traced part of the journey of Lewis and Clark, two hundred years after their landmark quest across the American continent, in our RV, I encouraged my children to imagine our journey as Lewis and Clark had done it—with no maps, no roads, no guides, and no food. "Imagine," I said to them, "the sheer determination of an expedition that had to surmount that level of obstacle!" How could they not be inspired by the lengths to which humans will go in their endless quest for knowledge? And how could they possibly whine for a DVD when they thought about what that trip would be like if they had to do it in a canoe!

#5: Help Them to See Their Own Power of Renewal

Perhaps most important, I want my kids to understand that they don't have to turn outside themselves for entertainment.

I want my children to understand that they always have, within themselves, the ability to make something new.

My daughter Mushki complained to me one day that she wasn't finding school very engaging. When I asked her what they'd talked about in class that day, she said one of her teachers was convinced that the tsunami in Southeast Asia and the devastation that Hurricane Katrina wreaked on the people of New Orleans were punishments from G-d. Mushki was shocked and dismayed: "I just can't believe she thinks it's okay to condemn hundreds of thousands of innocent people she's never even met! It's arrogant to imagine that you know what is in the mind of G-d!"

I asked her why she hadn't started this debate in class. "You claim to be bored, and yet you're sitting on the ability to turn that classroom into the site of a passionate debate about one of the most fundamental and interesting theological questions, a question that has engaged the faithful for centuries. If your teacher says something that you find completely outrageous—and I agree with you that condemning innocent people who suffer in a natural catastrophe as sinners is pretty darn unacceptable—then get up and challenge what's being said. Don't be afraid of your teacher, and don't be afraid to be out of step."

The next day, she respectfully engaged the teacher in debate, and the entire class joined in a discussion more lively than any they'd had in a long time. Mushki herself came home charged with a new passion and energy, a contagion that spread to our other children as they took up the question at dinner. Some difference from the listless boredom of the day before!

In a sense, Mushki had made herself a new girl. At school, she was faced with the same teacher, the same classmates, and the same four walls, but she had reached within herself, and initiated a different conversation. In so doing, she made the whole experience new again.

Every single one of us has the capacity to make the everyday new again, the same way Mushki did in her class. We do this not by acquiring more things, or better ones, but by plumbing the depths of the things that are already in our lives.

We can make everything in our lives new again, just by going deeper.

Nowhere is this more true than in our relationships. People are like the sea. They have depths that are obscured at the surface. I have been married for eighteen years, thank G-d, and I have only begun to scratch the surface of the complex and infinitely deep woman that I was blessed to marry. The same thing is true about my children, who continue to evolve and develop in endlessly surprising ways, and I have to get to know them every single day. If I miss even a day, there's a lot of catching up to do! Some parents never do, so their kids simply stop speaking to them. "You'll never understand me anyway."

We can't choose our parents, and we can't choose our kids. But we can choose to endlessly renew those relationships, so that they are never stale or boring. Want to know your kids? Plumb their depths. Get them to reveal themselves to you. Push when they don't want to be pushed. Don't give up. Never give in.

I hear, over and over, from dissatisfied parents that they can't get more than a monosyllable out of their children. I have to wonder—is the problem perhaps with the questions, which only skim the shallows? Instead of asking "How was school?" which is virtually guaranteed to elicit a stock, single-word response, try digging a little deeper. Ask because you're curious, not as a way of checking up, or because you feel like you should.

It doesn't have to be profound; instead of trotting out the tried and true, my friend Jean asked her daughter, "Did Mrs. Stein give you another pop quiz today?" She was shocked by the volubility of the response: "I can't believe her! Isabelle forgot her book in her locker last night, so she hadn't done the reading and she got really upset, but Mrs. Stein said it was okay and that she could write a paragraph on the new Harry Potter instead and take a different pop quiz tomorrow to make up, but she couldn't decide whether to write about Ron or Hermione." By asking just a slightly better, deeper question, Jean gave her daughter a different way of thinking about her day. Trivia? Maybe, but it gave Jean all the entrée she needed for a longer conversation about her daughter's immediate thoughts and concerns.

Another way to take your communication with your children to another level is by asking about—and sharing—things you've never discussed before. Your children think you're the same person every day, and indeed, that's probably very comforting to them. But how much do they really know about you? How much do they know about your own childhood, and what your hopes and dreams were then? How much do they know about how you felt about school, the books you remember liking (and hating), the disagreements you had with your own parents, the things that made you happy?

I tell my kids a lot of things about myself, more than most parents do, I suspect. They have always been fascinated by details of my own upbringing. They love hearing stories about my friends, my hobbies, the mistakes I made, and the things that turned me on. Now, I know that a lot of parents avoid those kinds of conversations because they fear being vulnerable in this way. They don't want to relive painful moments, or share their mistakes with their children, choosing instead to show their kids only those parts of them that have been thoroughly ironed out.

But I have always found that the best way to teach and to inspire is by personal example. So I feel that we have to overcome the discomfort and reveal ourselves to our children, showing them a depth that they may not have known we possessed. You'd be astonished by how much of a conversation starter an embarrassing story can be. . . .

And the complaint I hear most from kids—that their parents are like broken records, nagging in exactly the same way about exactly the same things—can also be solved with the same advice: go deeper. I've mentioned that my daughter Shterny was distracted in some of her classes this year. We have had a number of conversations about it, and I have tried to make every one different, examining a different dimension of the problem, so that it reaches her on a more profound level every time. If I say the same things over and over again, I'm just going to be nagging her—and she's just going to tune me out. But if I explore different facets of the same topic, I feel that she'll not only listen, but gain a deeper understanding of why I am concerned and of what she can do to help herself.

The first time, I simply reiterated my unconditional love for her. Another time, I took a different tack, saying, "The reason it's important to me that you do well in school is not because I'm worried about what college you'll go to, or what your teachers think. I couldn't care less what your teachers think; I am not from the school of thought that says teachers are always right.

"Rather, I want you to focus because I love you, and there's more of *you* in the world when you're concentrating. When you're looking out the window, part of you is lost out the window. But when you're concentrating on what you're doing, you're fully alive. Your daydreams pull you away from me, away from the world, and I want to feel your presence here. I don't want you to tread lightly in the world; I want your footprints to sink in deeply, so that you have a real impact. I don't care much about your grades, honestly. I have seen just as many C students succeed in later life as I have A students. I just want you to be fully present, because the world is impoverished without you."

It was a different conversation—same topic, perhaps, but from a wildly different direction. And it had an even more profound impression on her than the conversations we'd had before on the subject.

Keep your child's sense of wonder alive, and you give them a gift that keeps on giving. A child who has been encouraged to hold on to the precious facility of seeing the new in the everyday will never be bored with their world, but will rediscover new dimensions in every interaction. An ever-renewing sense of wonder will help them to be better, more satisfied husbands and wives. They'll get married and they'll *stay* married, because they won't need to hop in some new bed in order to find a new experience. They won't need to talk to their work colleagues to have a new conversation; their families will provide them with the stimulation they need.

Dare your children—and yourselves—to find the novelty in the everyday.

Tradition

Chapter Eleven

Tradition: Our Connection to Something Larger Than Ourselves

Children are not casual guests in our home. They
have been loaned to us temporarily for the purpose of
loving them and instilling a foundation of values on
which their future lives will be built.
—Dr. James C. Dobson

The PLANT method of parenting is about giving our kids roots, an unshakable foundation. But the best roots in the world are nothing without the warm sunshine of inspiration, which allows our children to grow up, turning their leaves toward the light.

Tradition, the fifth branch of the PLANT parenting method, reinforces both. Our traditions are an essential part of the foundation we give our children. They can provide them with an identity, a strong, indelible sense of themselves. Traditions can provide them with a community, a connection to a larger human network, which means that they will never be alone. But, perhaps most important, our traditions, provided that they are meaningful enough, can also give our children the ultimate inspiration: a sense of their place in the greater plan of the universe, an understanding of their cosmic purpose, and the irreplaceable role that they will play in bringing these traditions forward into the future.

Tradition . . . tradition. It's not just a throwaway line from *Fiddler on the Roof*. Rather, a sense of tradition strengthens the individual and the family, and never more than when the traditions connect your family to something bigger than itself.

TRADITION: A SOURCE OF IDENTITY

The first purpose of tradition is to give us an identity, a sense of who we are in the wider world.

Tradition gives us a sense of ourselves.

Too much of the pain in our lives happens when we don't have a secure identity, a knowledge of our deepest selves and of our unique place in the world. We've all had the sensation of being self-conscious, uncomfortable in our own skin. It's a profoundly unnerving feeling; you feel as if a spotlight has been focused on you, in order to highlight that you don't belong and haven't earned a place at the table. And this is particularly agonizing for children, whose identities are still being formed, which is why they often devote themselves to blending into their environment, for fear of being perceived as "different," or "weird."

Every one of us has to have something we can identify with, something that separates us out from the anonymous morass of people around us. It's not negotiable: we must know who we are. My beard and my yarmulke tell the world at large that I am a Jew; they are signifiers that tell everyone who sees me that I believe certain things and can be relied upon (hopefully!) to behave in a certain way. But they are more than that: the Jewish traditions I observe—whether the *tzitzis* (mini prayer shawl) I wear, the kosher food I eat, or the prayers I say—remind me that I have a commitment to G-d and to the principles that have been kept by the Jewish people since the dawn of civilization. This identity is central to who I am and defines my place among the nations.

A weak identity is the primary cause of human insecurity, and one of its foremost remedies is a strong sense of tradition.

The Talmud says that "a man without a home is not a man." Is this a statement of capitalism and property ownership? Of course not. It is a metaphor for an indelible inner identity. Here, "home" is a metaphysical term, not a physical one; it means the turf you have staked out that is yours and yours alone, unique to you, and impervious to change.

Some have their "home" on the outside. Their identity is defined by external factors: what they do, who they know, how they look, how much money or status or power they have. But they will always be subject to the winds of change— aging, a business reversal—because they have no idea who they really are on the inside. When you have a true home, a real identity, it travels with you wherever you go, and no matter what happens to you. Your identity never leaves you: you don't stop being Catholic when you're not sitting in a pew; you're don't stop being married when you're out of sight of your spouse; and you don't become a Spaniard just because you've gotten off the plane in Madrid. So your "home" is not one of brick and mortar, but one built of traditions and a sense of belonging.

Jewish lore tells of the silly inhabitants of the mythical city of Chelm. One day, one of those silly inhabitants went to the bathhouse, but he was afraid that, once he had taken off all his clothing, he would forget who he was. So he tied a red string on his big toe to remind him. In the course of soaping up, the red string came off his toe and found its way onto another man's toe. The man went to get dressed, saw that the red string was missing, and panicked. He then saw the red string on the other man's toe, and walked over to him: "Excuse me, sir; I know who you are. But can you please tell me who I am?"

The story, of course, is a metaphor for all those lost souls who make the mistake of defining themselves by external and changing circumstances. We must give our children a much more solid foundation upon which to base their identities, like the one that comes from being attached to a tradition and internalizing its substance.

I know this from personal experience. When I was fourteen years old, I left home to enroll in a rabbinical high school, three thousand miles from home. It was hard to be so far away from my family. I would go home to visit, get emotionally reattached to them, and dread having to leave them; then I would go to my Yeshiva, to my friends at the dorm, who were like a second family, and get all attached to that environment. I felt like a yo-yo, permanently lonely, and with no home. And when I would take those five-hour cross-country flights, I would look jealously at the married couples who traveled together. They, it seemed to me, brought their home with them on their travels, and I longed for the time when I could have that feeling.

In a sense, I was right: the tradition of marriage, of commitment, of fidelity, did give those people an identity and sense of belonging, so that their home was transformed from brick and mortar to flesh and blood. But I was also learning that I too brought my own home back and forth with me, in the form of my own traditions. I had made the decision to be a rabbi, responding to what I felt was an inner calling. My studies immersed me in a culture many thousands of years old, charging me with maintaining traditions that had sustained millions of my people. And the firmer my identity became, the more I realized that I didn't need anything external to feel comfortable and at home.

When you have a strong sense of yourself, you're always "home," even when you are far away.

What a gift this is to give to our children!

When that inner identity is strong, it provides a basis for all the decisions that you make in your life. In the third volume of Taylor Branch's magisterial biography of Martin Luther King, Jr., *At Canaan's Edge*, there is a story that perfectly illustrates this point. Reverend King called upon his friend, the great scholar and social activist Rabbi Abraham Joshua Heschel, to join him on the now-legendary march from Selma to Montgomery in March 1965. Heschel was torn. On the one hand, he wished to participate in an enterprise he considered to be G-d's work. But the march was to begin on Saturday, the Sabbath, and there are all kinds of restrictions on work and movement on the Sabbath that Heschel could not ignore.

So he found ways to march that also honored the Sabbath. He came to Selma before the Sabbath began, he ate only kosher foods—a challenge in Selma in 1965, to be sure!—and he made sure only to walk, even when his feet became incredibly tired, because of the Sabbath prohibition of riding in a car.

The story inspires me, even as I retell it: as Rabbi Heschel did this immensely powerful good deed, *he did it as a Jew*. As he marched to change the evil practice of segregation with his black brothers and sisters, he brought his own traditions—the source of the values that led him to march.

There are few things as sad as a person without a clearly defined sense of self. These tragic people are chameleons, destined to wander in a kind of purgatory, changing their allegiances with no underlying sense of loyalty to themselves or to the traditions in which they were raised. We cannot abandon our children to such a fate. It is true that the Jewish people are some of the most persecuted in the world, and unlike African Americans, Jews can "pass" as something we are not. We can take off our yarmulkes, change our names, shave our beards, and get baptized. But most of us choose not to, because when we turn our backs on our traditions, something infinitely precious is lost. An identity is only secure when it is something that you wear with pride.

This is why I was surprised to see an article in *USA Today* after the first war in Iraq advising Americans to dodge anti-American sentiment abroad by not "flaunting" American symbols like the Stars and Stripes on a T-shirt. I read the story to my children with a real sense of outrage. We have to encourage Americans to be proud of who they are *wherever* they are, in *all* circumstances. You can't shed your identity when it's convenient—and when you consider the tradition of freedom, democracy, and initiative that our flag represents, it truly is reprehensible to conceal your alliance with that tradition just because it's going to make it harder to get a taxi in Italy.

I love being an American, and being an American is the source of many of the traditions I hold most dear. For the eleven years I lived in Europe, the knowledge that I came from a country that honors hard work and individual effort over hereditary nobility allowed me to stand my ground with everyone I met, from royalty on down. I hosted and met many of the world's greatest leaders at Oxford, and with rare exceptions, I never felt inferior to them, and part of my confidence came from knowing that I was the unofficial representative of a culture that believes that man is the governor of his own destiny, the product of his own toil, not the arbitrary recipient of a title or a "good" last name. And by instilling this uniquely American sense of identity in my children, I hope to ensure that they never feel inferior to any man or woman as well.

I can think of nothing of greater value or lasting permanence that we can give our children than the solid sense of themselves that comes from a strong inner identity. I consider it my mission to give my children a sense of who they are in the world that will last them a lifetime.

And trust me, that strong sense of identity *is* something you get from your parents. Your child has her own personality, likes and dislikes, but she will get her identity from the richness of the traditions you raise her with. In this way, your identity is like a name. My parents gave me the name Shmuley and it has become an integral part of me, inseparable from the way I think about myself. I am Shmuley, and Shmuley is me. Names are not arbitrary; they are carefully chosen by parents for their children, and identities are the same. They must also be calculated, planned, and built from the ground up, because only then can we successfully give our children a sense of who they are.

I love it when I hear the little kids telling each other that we're going to Florida, say, three *Shabboses* from now, as opposed to three weeks. It may seem like a small thing, but it's how I know that this tradition that is so important to me is also central to their lives, so that it affects even the way they understand the passage of time. A proud moment of early fatherhood came when one of my friends brought my (then) three-year-old daughter back from his own daughter's birthday party and told me this story: They had handed out lollipops as party favors when it was time to go; my daughter, the only Jewish girl there, asked if they were kosher. When it turned out they were not, she said, "I guess I'd better not have one, then." It not only vindicated the many efforts my wife and I have made to raise religious children in a secular world, but demonstrated exactly why we do it: because when you're Jewish, what you can and cannot eat reminds you of *who you are*.

And the sense of identity that you get from being rooted in a particular tradition can be a lifesaver for a young man or woman when they embark on the journey—as all adolescents do—of discovering exactly who they are. Certainly, one of the biggest problems facing children today is peer pressure, the pressure to conform, to do what everyone else is doing. But when you know right from wrong because of the traditions you were raised in, and when your inner self has been forged in the fire of those traditions so that it is as strong as iron, it's easier to say no to a persistent boy or the offer of a joint.

Adults underestimate peer pressure, because we have a more firmly defined sense of ourselves. Our longer lives have taught us that it's better to be grounded for two weeks than to be found dead beside a drunk driver, and most of us have enough confidence to throw back a fish who's telling us he'll sleep with our best friend if we don't capitulate to his requests for sex. But most teenagers don't yet have a solid sense of themselves, so they look outside themselves—to the culture, to their friends, to their boyfriends and girlfriends—for affirmation and direction.

When religion or a strong sense of tradition is part of that mix, it increases the likelihood that they'll make the right choice—as opposed to one that's "right now." I'm not sure that we can ever counteract the power of peer pressure completely, but making sure that our children have a solid backing in tradition gives them something to fall back on, a presence at their center instead of a void that only someone outside can fill. My daughters know that religious Jewish girls don't socialize with boys and don't date recreationally. To do so would be to go against their sense of self, and so they say no when a group of their friends is going to hang out with boys at the mall. Their tradition, a tradition they have internalized, is to respect the ideals of love, romance, and sex within the context of the sacred commitment of marriage. It helps them to define who they are, and how they are different from other teenagers, like those whose parents believe that experience—even the very harmful type—is the best teacher.

TRADITION STRENGTHENS OUR BOND TO ONE ANOTHER

No matter where I am in this world, I know that I can find a place to celebrate the Sabbath. I am part of a larger Jewish family, and my membership in that group means that strangers will open their home to me, feed me, give me a place to pray and to sleep. Once, when I was traveling back from a book tour in Australia, my flight was forced to land in Singapore and I got stuck out there for the Sabbath. I called the local rabbi, who invited me—sight unseen—into his home. He fed me, inspired me, put me up for the night, and asked me to lecture in his synagogue the next day. Even though we were strangers, we were still family. We are part of a single community, members of the Jewish nation.

Tradition is not just important because of the strength it confers on the individual, but because our traditions connect us to a larger human network.

Our traditions mean that we are never truly alone.

Next to having a strong sense of self, I can think of nothing more important than eradicating the feeling that we are alone in the world. There is nothing more toxic and painful than loneliness; no greater source of human distress than the feeling that we are abandoned and forlorn. In fact, it is the very first thing that G-d speaks out against in the Bible, the very first thing He calls bad: "It is not good for man to be alone."

There are three levels of loneliness—and a life of traditions is instrumental in alleviating all three of them. The first level of loneliness is the simple need to be around people. We all need human contact, even if it's superficial. Why else do we make small talk at the water cooler, or in the men's room? People who live or work by themselves will often stop by a sports bar or a Starbucks; just sitting in the company of the other regulars can right the feeling of being isolated and out of sync that comes from being too long alone. It may not be intimacy, but it satisfies this very first level of loneliness—because it's not a deep need; even a relatively shallow tradition like the American hobby of watching baseball can alleviate it. The first level of human loneliness is addressed through community, through everyday communal interactions.

The second level of loneliness is more profound. The ancient rabbis asked a very good question about Adam, alone in the Garden of Eden: surrounded as he was by animals, angels, and G-d Himself, why was Adam lonely? I find their answer ingenious: Adam felt lonely *because he wasn't needed.* The animals were self-sufficient, and G-d and the angels were perfect. Perfect beings have no needs; they could enjoy Adam, hang out with him and have a figurative beer, but they did not *need* him. No angel came to Adam and asked to be comforted for the loss of a child. No celestial creature came to Adam with financial troubles and a request for a loan.

It was only when Eve arrived—another imperfect being like himself who needed to be listened to and comforted, hugged and held, complimented and appreciated—by him!—that Adam felt truly complete. He was now not just a creature to hang out with, but a *necessary* one. This second level of loneliness can be ameliorated with family traditions, something we will talk more about in the next chapter.

All the things we do to support our traditions, we do together as a family and as a community.

Think of the midday dinner that most Christians have after church on Sundays; it's a tradition celebrated around the world. Whether you're having ackee and saltfish or pot roast, you're spending a few hours sitting with your family, talking and breaking bread. You're wanted, you're known—and you're irreplaceable. Many people believe that John F. Kennedy was the most inspiring president of the last century, but only minutes after his death, Lyndon Johnson was sworn in as his replacement as the President of the United States. The country could replace Kennedy, but his family couldn't; even though his wife remarried, she is buried next to him in Arlington National Cemetery, and she never truly recovered from his loss. This truth is what holds families together, and it's when it stops being true that families fall apart. The number-one reason I hear from wives who are contemplating leaving their husbands is that they no longer feel needed; their husbands no longer confide in them, no longer turn to them for comfort. So the second level of human loneliness is assuaged through a commitment to family.

The third level of loneliness is the deepest of all. It is the fear that you will never be truly understood. The knowledge that we are all individuals is a blessing, but it can also be a curse if it makes you feel that you are cut off from others. That is the paradox of human existence. On the one hand, we are all special because we are individuals, unique and irreplaceable. On the other hand, this guarantees that on the deepest of all levels we will forever be lonely. No one can ever fully understand who we are without actually becoming us. Indeed, this paradox is fully in evidence in the institution of marriage: what makes us love another person is his or her difference. Real physical and emotional intimacy helps us to breach these differences, but there will always be a fundamental difference between you. So while you love each other and can comfort each other, the ultimate success of the marriage is dependent on *never* fully understanding each other.

There is a famous saying of the ancient Kabbalists regarding the relationship between G-d and man. It says, "If I were to really understand G-d, then I would be G-d." The same is true of our spouses. The only way to really understand them is to become them. And if we were to become them, the marriages would be over because they would no longer *need* us and we would no longer be interesting to them. Another human being can never "get you" fully—they can love you, they can comfort you, they can even appreciate you, but they can't ever fully understand what it means to *be* you, to walk in your shoes and to experience your individual dreams, disappointments, and celebrations.

This is why we pray. The only Being that can truly "get" us is G-d. No one can truly understand us or fathom our depths except He who created us. So it is this level of loneliness that our religious traditions address—they connect us to

G-d, who knows everything, and knows every one of us completely. When I pray, I believe I am talking to G-d, and that no matter how alone I am in the world, He is always with me. As Maya Angelou has said, "Of all the needs (there are none imaginary) a lonely child has, the one that must be satisfied, if there is going to be hope and a hope of wholeness, is the unshaken need for an unshakable God." So the last and deepest level of loneliness is assuaged through connection to G-d and religious tradition.

So here you have the three levels of loneliness and their three remedies: traditions that support the communal, the familial, and the divine. I can't think of any benefaction we can give our children that is more important than knowing they will not have to suffer through a disconnected life, feeling forlorn and alone.

TRADITION GIVES US A SENSE OF PURPOSE

Many of the parents I speak to are shocked by their children's listlessness. This is especially true of the baby boomers I talk to, many of whom spent their adolescence and early adulthood working for social justice. They remember their youth as a time of passion and politics—a time when they would have sacrificed everything, including their very safety, to make the world a slightly better place. How can their own children be content to sit on the sidelines, playing video games and listening to pop music?

It is fascinating to think about how hard those young people worked in the 1960s, under such pressure and for such little immediate gain. But they had something better: they knew that they stood, with their country, at the dawn of a new era. The strength of their convictions fueled their ability to sacrifice and their desire to fight.

It does not seem accidental to me that so many powerful social movements—like the civil rights movement in this country—come out of a religious tradition such as the black churches of the American South. When you understand that you are one of G-d's children, it adds an additional layer to your identity, and you gain a unique sense of yourself. The unconditional love we show our children gives them a secure foundation. No wonder that G-d's love—the ultimate expression of unconditional love—is that much more empowering, and gives them an even stronger sense of purpose.

But tradition isn't exclusively the province of the religious. Even if you do not believe in G-d—or aren't sure—you can still believe that there is a moral order to the universe, and that every human being has a responsibility to act in a way that is generous and righteous, purposeful and meaningful. Even if you aren't that religious, I bet you believe that human life is precious, even sacred, and that every individual is necessary and special, playing a vital role in the unfolding of human events. Even if you're not religious, you probably still believe in selflessness and sacrifice and a life of transcendence. You accept that what goes around comes around, that crime doesn't pay, and that being stingy with your money or your love will ultimately cause the whole earth to shrink.

These beliefs, these traditions, are not the exclusive preserve of the religious—and they are extremely important concepts to convey to your children. Even nonreligious traditions can be very effective in strengthening the family bond, and in giving our children a feeling of being connected to other human beings and to a moral force in the universe.

Our children today lack a sense of purpose, and they suffer terribly as a result. As Viktor Frankel, the celebrated Holocaust survivor and therapist, insightfully observed, mental illness results primarily from a feeling of purposelessness. **Children *need* meaning in order to be mentally and emotionally healthy.**

But our children don't see that their lives are going anywhere; they don't feel that they have anything unique to contribute, or that they are part of a larger, more ornate plan. I know, because I was one of those children.

When I was thirteen years old, I had a private audience with the Lubavitcher Rebbe, Rabbi Menachem Schneerson. A private audience was tremendously difficult to arrange; an older rabbinical student who had taken me under his wing had pulled strings to make it happen. I owe him to this day, because that meeting changed my life. I was a cynical child of divorce who was doing poorly at school. I was aimless and adrift, and I didn't see myself as anything special. Looking back now, I realize that I lacked guidance, and that crucial ingredient: inspiration.

I wrote as much to the rebbe in a long letter, which I put into the palm of his hand when I walked into his office at 3:30 a.m.—the rebbe tirelessly worked to run his global educational organization all day, and then gave people private audiences all night. He read my letter, took out a tiny pencil, and circled certain passages. He looked up at me with penetrating blue eyes and asked me a few questions. Then he spoke, and I felt that he did so in complete sincerity, and with an immediate, intimate knowledge of my inner self that few others have ever achieved. He said, "I bless you today, that you will grow to be a light to your family, your school, the Jewish people, and the entire world."

I felt chills up and down my spine, and walked out of his office quite literally transformed. I had walked in as a boy who perceived his life as a series of accidents. But in a brief meeting, lasting all of three minutes and thirty-three seconds, I walked out with a sense of purpose. I had a reason to live: to be a light in the world, to increase the planet's luminescence. I finally understood that I had been designed with a purpose, and that purpose was not to be broken, but to heal—both myself and others. Knowing this purpose gave me the strength I needed not to be prisoner to my own wounds, but to live free. From that moment on, I sought connectivity, not isolation. I made every attempt to devote myself to others.

That, for me, is the power of religion's sense of spiritual purposefulness, and it is yet another reason that it is so very important to raise our children with strong traditions. They must understand that their existence has a purpose, that what they have to offer is singular and valuable. They must understand that they are connected to everyone who has come before them, and to everyone who celebrates those traditions in the world today.

In the same way that children flourish when they are part of the network of a family, they benefit greatly from knowing that they are connected to those who have gone before us. When my children light the candles for Chanukah, they are connected at that moment not only to the glorious Macca-bees who inflicted catastrophic defeat against pagan Greek armies ten times their size, but to all Jewish children every-where who have ever stood at the menorah in an attempt to bring light to the world. When the youngest child in our home asks the Four Questions at our Passover seder, he is connected to every Jewish child who has ever asked those questions.

And there is no inspiration greater than knowing that they are an essential part of carrying that tradition forward. This is how I explain tradition to my children: I tell them that every individual is a link in a higher chain of existence. The chain is only as strong as each individual link. What will your contribution be? Will you make the chain stronger, or will you sever it? The continuity of that tradition is depen-dent entirely on them.

Giving our children a tradition makes them feel like they're the guardians of an ancient heirloom; the torch has been passed for them to protect. By teaching our children that they are an essential link in an unbroken chain of tradition, we are really telling them the two most important words in the entire vocabulary of parenting: *you matter.* Whether you were born or not matters. Whether you live or die matters. Whether you develop your potential matters. Whether you contribute your unique gift to the world matters. And every-thing rests on your decision: whether you will bring new life to an ancient tradition, or allow it to atrophy. You have no idea how significant your existence is—now you must rise to the challenge.

When Pat Tillman was called to serve in Afghanistan,

he could have said, "Let somebody else go." He had been a celebrity athlete, leading the good life, and had given up a $3 million contract in the NFL to enlist in the army. He understood that he was needed on the front line, defending American democracy against terrorism. And we lost him as he tried to protect it—just as we lost 58,000 people in Vietnam, just as Patrick Henry declared, "Give me liberty or give me death," just as the greatest generation fought against Hitler and indomitable marines stormed the beaches at Iwo Jima. The continuity of the American way of life rested, for a moment, on the shoulders of Pat Tillman, and he was there to answer the call. And while *he* was lost, the American tradition of liberty that he died to defend grew stronger as a result.

I tell my children the same thing about their Jewish traditions: we have been called to defend monotheism and the Ten Commandments, and to witness G-d's presence in history. As the keepers of that tradition, we have been subject to unceasing violence—pogroms, inquisitions, expulsions, auto-da-fés, crusades, and the Holocaust. But even as six million men, women, and children were gassed because of their identity, they never severed their connection to G-d or denied their tradition. Now, I tell my children, the legacy of that commitment is in your hands. You're the link.

I know how powerful an inspiration this can be, because it has been so in my own life. I have had professional ups and downs, like everyone else in the world, but I have never doubted for a second that I need to push forward to do the work I do. Jews believe in the concept of *tikkun olam*, the idea that every one of us has a personal responsibility to heal the world through social action and justice. I see the work I do to strengthen couples and families in crisis as part of G-d's plan to repair the world. The Talmud says that G-d weeps after every divorce, and I endeavor my utmost to cease those celestial tears. I have dedicated my career to trying to open Judaism up a little bit, to emphasize its universal components so that its light and wisdom can contribute to the healing of our lives. My traditions bolster me when I feel weak or unsure, and I wouldn't dream of raising my children without a similar understanding of their role in this world.

I keep the Sabbath primarily because I love G-d and it is His holy day, but also because I want my life to be a living example of the ancient traditions that I hold dear, and that I wish my children to emulate. And I am emboldened and enlivened by the surge of inspiration that comes from being a standard-bearer, from keeping something infinitely important alive.

TRADITION

CHAPTER TWELVE

Strengthen Your Family:
Establish Your Own Traditions

Family life is full of major and minor crises—the ups and
downs of health, success and failure in career, marriage, and
divorce—and all kinds of characters. It is tied to places
and events and histories. With all of these felt details, life
etches itself into memory and personality. It's difficult to
imagine anything more nourishing to the soul.

—Thomas Moore

I think you'll be pleasantly surprised to discover how easy it
is to establish traditions in your own home.

Children are natural tradition keepers—they have an in-
herent love of the familiar and the routine. It not only makes
them feel safe, but knowing what is going to happen next helps
them to participate more fully in the events. They love having
an identity (you can see this in the way they gather information about themselves, like their favorite colors and their favorite foods, even when they are very young). They love being

connected to and feeling at one with a community. And they cannot help but be inspired by the responsibility conferred upon them as they carry their traditions into the future.

A WORD OF CAUTION

The type of traditions you choose to reinforce in your family is important; it's not enough simply to have them.

First of all, it must be something with meaning. Although there will undoubtedly be something very comforting and nice about your children knowing that every Friday is pizza night, it lacks the kind of depth that will have a true impact on their characters.

More seriously, I think too many people trap their sons and daughters in traditions that don't matter. They give them tradition, but the wrong traditions—meaningless ones. There's nothing wrong with wanting your daughter to go to Radcliffe, like you did and your mother and grandmother before you, but that's not the kind of tradition that I suggest you instill in your children.

Where you go to college, or what you do for a living, is a *secondary* identity, not a primary one.

Perhaps your son will become a doctor, as all the men in your family have before him. But even if he does, he won't be a doctor at the very core of his soul, he'll merely practice medicine. The other traditions you give him will last: he will, for instance, always be a beloved son, a Catholic, and a Puerto Rican, but he will stop being a doctor when he leaves his white coat on the back of the office door.

It's not simply that these shallower traditions are not rich enough to sustain our children; I think they are dangerous in their own right. Teaching our children that their identity comes from the outside rather than from the inside—from things they do rather than the things they *are*—will make them weak, not strong. It will make them increasingly dependent on those external things until they become desperate to hold on to them.

Isn't this overidentification with externals behind so many of the maladies that rip the American family apart? The workaholism, the materialism, the eating disorders, the adultery? A workaholic defines his worth as a human being by his productivity and his social status; the adulterous husband defines his worth by how many women are interested in him. The bulimic derives her self-worth from her dress size, the materialist from her designer shoes and homes. All of them are incapable of finding a sense of real identity and satisfaction from within.

So when we condition our children to define themselves by external traditions, like the schools they get into or the jobs they succeed in, this kind of tradition becomes a prison, not a benediction.

Our traditions should have the power to uplift us, through a tremendous sense of purpose and meaningfulness.

This is one of the reasons I love raising Jewish children. Participating in the traditions of Judaism tells my children, in a way that I never could, that their lives are not accidental and their existence is not capricious. Rather, they are part of something glorious, something noble, something eternal—and that knowledge directly affects the way they behave. But you don't have to be Jewish to experience that. You just need to be part of a tradition.

When our children feel connected to something larger than themselves, they understand that what they do really matters.

Judaism reinforces for my children the idea that they are beloved because of their unique spiritual talents, and it promotes values that I cherish as a result. Being Jewish reinforces my children's humanity, not their spending power; it rewards them for what they think and do, not because of how they look. Getting positive reinforcement for the purity of their thought and the charity of their gestures is a powerful counterpoint to the cynicism that sets in around middle school, when children begin to understand that they are joining a world that cares much more for their bodies than for their souls.

Obviously, Judaism is not the only way. In order to find the traditions that will work for you and your family, I would simply encourage you to get in touch once again with your passions, whatever you feel connects you and your family to something larger in the world and to the divine. No doubt you too have values that you cherish, things that connect you to the world at large, and define who you are. Give your children those same definitions.

What are the things that inspire you, and what activities can help your children internalize those ideals? For me, traditions fall into three main categories: familial, national, and religious.

FAMILY TRADITIONS

Most of us in search of tradition don't have to look much further than our own families. Young children are often surprised to discover that older people struggled with many of the same things they struggle with in their daily lives. At a recent dinner in our home, my daughters were transfixed by the story of a fraught courtship—no matter that the guest telling the story was in her seventies, and the events she was describing had taken place fifty years before.

I make sure that my children spend as much time as possible with our extended family, simply so that they can hear the family story. Certainly, knowing about the traditions and values held by my forefathers has greatly influenced my own choices. My grandfather had thirteen children, and very little money. He was known for saying that his treasures were his children. I grew up knowing this, and knowing' that in our family it is a tradition to cherish children—the more the merrier. This is a tradition I am proud to continue with my wife, and one for which we thank G-d. And the fact that I am the father of many kids has become a real part of my identity.

America is made up of people who came—at one time or another—from other places, and many of them brought their own unique customs and values with them. How much do your children know about what your parents (or you, or your parents' parents) brought to this country? For many children, simply learning these stories helps to connect them to a tradition.

My friend Amelia spends Sunday afternoons making the rich German pastries of her youth with her granddaughter

Tracy. They talk while they bake strudel, kuchen, and babka, just as a younger Amelia bonded with her own grandmother, who was killed—along with much of the rest of her family—in the Holocaust. It gives my friend great pleasure to see that her granddaughter, now eleven, no longer needs the recipe cards.

But this simple tradition is more than butter and sugar. Tracy takes the leftover pastries to share with her friends at school, and in so doing, she shares with them another dimension of her life. As a result, they now see her not just as someone who likes the blond member of the boy band as opposed to the dark-haired one, but as someone who has a family, a nationality, and a religion. And of course it's natural for her to share some of her grandmother's stories while they snack, so that this group of eleven-year-old girls in Connecticut now have a connection, in the form of a firsthand account of a survivor's experience in the death camps, to the horrifying events of the last century.

And Amelia knows that, long after she is gone, Tracy will share their Sunday morning tradition with her own children and grandchildren. That's powerful cake!

Even the smallest thing can become a tradition if it is rooted in a larger moral understanding of the world. I have made it a habit in my life, for instance, to try never to pass a destitute person without giving him some money. It doesn't matter if I'm late, or if there's no change in my pockets, or if my arms are filled with books and my laptop. I still try to stop and give a dollar and a smile, and to say, "G-d bless you." I don't always succeed. But I do try.

I don't imagine that I'm single-handedly eradicating poverty, but I give for two simple reasons: first, because the person who is asking is a child of G-d, a human brother, who is in distress; second, because that little dollar, while not really a lot of money, represents a lot of dignity. By giving to those who are tragically reduced to asking, I can show them that they are important enough to me that I am willing to disrupt my day for them. Walking by someone who has been reduced to asking for help would tell that person that he doesn't matter, that he's invisible, and it would rob him of the last shred of his dignity. And when I talk to my children about this obligation, I make it clear that I feel that helping other people to maintain their dignity is the thing I most believe in.

It may sound like an odd sort of tradition, but I noticed, waiting for two of my daughters to join me in a restaurant, that my children have picked it up. So this is another tradition—a highly important one, I feel—that I have been able to impart to my kids.

Charity in general is a great tradition to establish with your family. One of my friends has developed a relationship with the nursing home in his neighborhood; he, his four kids, and their gentle Labrador retriever spend one Sunday afternoon a month visiting with the elderly people there. Another family I know dedicate their Thanksgiving Day to cooking and serving dinner at a homeless shelter. Another family I met at the park trains dogs to work with people with disabilities. The children get their dearest wish (a puppy!) and the simplest household chore—taking the dog for a walk—is elevated into something with much more significance.

A daughter and mother I know run the same 5K race every year to raise money for breast cancer, a disease that has devastated the women on both sides of their family. Training together, running the race, and celebrating afterward has become a meaningful and charitable tradition, not to mention a lovely (and healthful) way to spend time together.

I was raised by my mother in a highly ecumenical tradition of openness to all religions, races, and walks of life. Though we were a religious Jewish family, we regularly had non-Jewish guests at our Sabbath table. My mother truly treated all humanity as if they were her brothers and sisters, and she does to this very day. I have tried to communicate those values to my own children. At our Sabbath table, there are always people of many different backgrounds. If my children are color-blind and without prejudice, it's not because they've been told to respect all of G-d's children, no matter what they look like or believe; it's because they have been exposed to people with wildly different backgrounds for all their lives and have relished their company.

Perhaps some of these examples will encourage you to find some traditions that you and your family can participate in to bring you together as a family. Don't be afraid to start small. As far as I'm concerned, one of the most important traditions that threatens to fall by the wayside in contemporary American life is one of the most simple: the family dinner. Kids have so many extracurricular activities that it's impossible to synchronize their different schedules, while their parents stay late at work, or grab something from the kitchen on their way to the home office to catch up on reading or e-mail. I know more than one family that simply keeps a large casserole in the oven at low heat for the entire evening; as the various family members roll in, they grab a plate, dish themselves up some food, and disappear again to their disparate activities.

I find this image almost intolerably lonely. To be sure, my family doesn't have dinner together every night, but we have dinner together most nights, and it is one of the greatest simple pleasures of my life. It may not always be a leisurely banquet—there is homework to do and e-mail to answer in our house, too—but everyone in the family is in a seat at the same time for at least a half hour.

And I do my very best to make this time count. Some of the Christian families I've dined with make it a habit to go around the table so that each family member can say something they're grateful for—a tradition I find delightful. We Jews have a similar tradition which I practice at my own table in the form of asking each guest to say a l'chaim, a toast to some aspect of life. But no matter what, I consider it to be my job to keep the conversation interesting—and inspirational.

So at our house, there's no desultory "How was your day?" stuff. It's rare that we don't throw some topic out for discussion—we'll solicit our children's opinions on a major news story, for instance, or something that has come up over the course of one of our days. I'll throw trivia at them, or tell jokes. And it's not just the Shmuley Hour; once your children become acclimatized to a tradition like this one, they will also begin to contribute. The older ones especially will use time at the table as a clearinghouse for their own concerns or opinions about something happening in the world at large or at school, while the younger ones will take the opportunity to show off a piece of art they've made or something new they've learned or done.

What you eat isn't important—take-out Chinese can be just as inspirational as coq au vin. And it doesn't have to be every night—start with once or twice a week! Even what you talk about isn't ultimately that important, as long as everyone is there and participating. But establishing a regular time to be together around a table is a family tradition that every family in America can—and should—start tonight.

NATIONAL TRADITIONS

Although religious traditions dominate in my house, they are certainly not the only ones we observe. As you have already gathered, I am a very proud American, amazed at my good fortune to live in this miraculous and glorious country.

As far as I'm concerned, the two traditions are not entirely separate. America is a country with a deep-seated faith and love for the Creator, the only country on earth where G-d's name appears on the currency. And it is a country that is deeply blessed by the Creator as well. But it is also a country that nobly challenged and rejected the European fallacy that some human beings are born more worthy than others. What could possibly be more inspiring to a child than the story of an upstart country fighting against an established one for the right to self-determination? And America has grown into a country that believes its wealth and power should be devoted to freedom worldwide, and one that risks both blood and treasure for the freedom of others.

I try to communicate all this to my children, so that their own love of country equals and exceeds my own. As you know, we have made a family tradition out of going to historical sites. I have taken my children to Revolutionary and Civil War battlefields all across the nation, explaining to them the nature of the conflict that took place on that sacred ground. From the triumph of Saratoga and Yorktown to the bloodied fields of Gettysburg and Vicksburg, I want my children to understand that brave Americans fought and died for principles that were sacred to the republic. In the case of the Revolutionary War, it was a belief in the rights of every human being to liberty and self-determination. In the case of the Northern soldiers in the Civil War, it was a belief that America was too special a country to be torn asunder over any rift, and too great a country to betray its founding ideals by enslaving any man, woman, or child.

I take my kids to Washington, DC, as often as I can. We have walked late at night amid the haunting silence of the Vietnam War Memorial and stood hushed in front of the giant statue of the saintly Abraham Lincoln. I have tried to convey to them a sense of the majesty of the Iwo Jima Marine Memorial and the courage of men who stormed beaches and let their blood run like rivers in order to turn back the tide of tyranny. Through all of this, my objective is to instill within my children a love for American tradition and the democratic, freedom-loving values this country has always cherished.

We also make traditions out of celebrating the astonishing range of natural beauty that this country has to offer. We have made hiking to rivers and lakes a family tradition in the warmer months, and skiing in the mountains in the winter. Scuba diving is becoming another tradition. These are activities we do together, which strengthens our family. And it is my hope that these activities also teach my children that loving nature means coexisting with it, not dominating or profiting from it.

Nations come with their own traditions, and holidays to celebrate them. Presidents' Day, Labor Day, Veterans Day— are these just an excuse for your kids not to go to school, and for you to take a day off work? Or do you take a moment to really commemorate the tremendous sacrifices that these days are designed to capture? We watch the fireworks and eat hot dogs with everyone else on Independence Day, but I try to combine that day with a visit to a historical site or at least a story to make sure that my children really take a moment to understand what tremendous achievements the country is celebrating. And nothing is more American than Thanksgiving dinner. I love living in a country that takes a whole day to show gratitude to G-d for something as simple as food. That's why I celebrated Thanksgiving at Oxford, so that the American students there would have a place to give thanks and our British friends could be inspired by our tradition to join us at the table and show gratitude for something we unfortunately take for granted all the other days of the year.

Don't get me wrong: not all the American traditions we celebrate are so lofty. Every year, we have a Super Bowl party, complete with friends and buckets of nosh. The kids and I go shopping, throwing the worst junk in the supermarket into the cart; then we go home and jump up and down and yell at the television, like everyone else. This may not be the most important tradition we celebrate—but just because making my wife laugh isn't as important a value as fidelity doesn't mean that I shouldn't try to do it every once in a while. When it comes to tradition, even the trivial can sometimes be important.

RELIGIOUS TRADITIONS

I believe that a spiritual or religious tradition is a necessity for children, not a luxury. By giving our children a religious tradition within which to anchor their lives, we teach our children one of life's greatest lessons: that the most precious things are specifically those that cannot be seen, touched, held, or acquired. Cars, clothes, and MP3 players are not life's most valuable commodities, contrary to what Madison Avenue would have you believe. These things are transient and they corrode. But there are other things, infinite things, so transcendent that they cannot be apprehended by the senses. These things, like G-d and love, require us to reach higher, and it is to those things that we should be devoting our lives.

Above all else, a religious tradition instills the kinds of values that strongly contribute not only to our ability to raise great kids—kids who are confident, secure, and purposeful— but to raising kids who strive to make the world a better place. For instance, Judaism teaches children that their every action counts, and that nothing they do is ever insignificant. It teaches them that their existence was called forth by G-d Almighty for a glorious purpose. They are not an accident of nature, but were given a special gift to share with the world, which it would be a crime against the universe to squander. They learn that a single good deed can bring the entire world into redemption.

Religion gives us a set of ready-made traditions that support a larger tradition. Obviously, the tradition within which I have raised my own children is Orthodox Judaism. It is important to me that they have a solid grounding in their Jewish heritage and customs, and that they live by the Jewish values of holiness, community, charity, hospitality, and humanity. Within the greater tradition of Orthodox Jewry come many smaller traditions that are an intrinsic part of our lives: we study the Bible daily, pray three times a day, observe biblical festivals, have mezuzahs on our doors, and keep a strictly kosher home.

Of course, one of the most important traditions in religious Jewish life is the celebration of the Sabbath, the creative pause, sanctified by the divine example of God ceasing in His labors after creating the universe. I believe that the Sabbath is one of the greatest spiritual and social contributions to civilization, not least because of what it does to strengthen the bonds between family members. For twenty-four hours, we are prohibited from doing any work. We are prohibited from using electricity, from writing, from driving, from cooking, from doing anything that represents creative labor.

That's a lot of prohibition for twenty-four hours, right? But out of those restrictions come an amazing sense of the significance of the truly important things in our lives. Nature has our full attention, because we are prohibited from driving and must walk if we want to go somewhere. All the warmth, kinship, and love we get from family and our neighbors have our full attention. G-d has our full attention. It's a higher sense of reality—one that celebrates everything that is real and everlasting, and dismisses all that is illusory or ephemeral or empty.

I know a number of Christian families—and indeed, a few secular ones—who have created their own version of the Sabbath. They turn off their phones, close their laptops, hide the remote, and ignore the ringing of the phone. They spend the time together, interacting face-to-face, as families should. If they are religious, they might read the Bible together. If not, they go for long walks, make meals together, play games, or read. These days without distractions give them the space to talk about what is most meaningful to them, and the opportunity to reconnect with those values. They go back to the hustle and bustle of their weeks feeling more attached to one another, and to the ideals they wish to uphold.

Our religious traditions bring us together and help us to celebrate the values most important to us. But there is a practical aspect as well to educating our children in a religious tradition. The stories that come from our religious traditions shed light on the trials and tribulations of our own times, and they can help guide our behavior—something very important for children, who have less life experience to draw upon when they're making decisions. I don't simply tell my kids bedtime stories, but stories of saintly rabbis and the righteous lives of courage, charity, and scholarship they led. I tell them stories of the sacrifice of Jewish martyrs through the ages, and what men and women have been prepared to do simply to hold on to their beliefs since the beginning of time. I tell them stories of the civil rights struggle and the greatness of men like the Reverend Martin Luther King, Jr., who faced character assassination, and then real assassination, as he strove to establish the biblical principle of all men created in the divine image.

These stories can have a profound effect on a child, an influence that will continue to be heard well into adulthood. When I was a kid in camp myself, when I was about ten years old, my counselor told me the story of Rabbi Israel Baal Shem Tov, the great founder of the Hassidic Jewish movement in Russia, who lived in the seventeenth century. Orphaned as a young boy, he made a point of walking every night deep into the forest all by himself. The villagers thought him strange, and wondered why he did this, and he responded, "I am training myself to fear none but G-d alone." You cannot imagine how powerful an impression this had on me—and although I first heard it thirty years ago, I still think about it when I find myself afraid. When I tell my children this story, I remind them that they have no reason to be afraid of anyone or anything; there is nothing that can defeat them, other than betraying their own sense of right and wrong.

There is tremendous pride for me in watching my children join the religious tradition that has meant so much to me in my own life. I love watching my children as I read them the story of Job. I can see that they are conflicted—what a miserable life he had even though he was righteous! Like all the others who came before them, they must wrestle with how a just G-d can allow so much undeserved suffering. I love watching them on Yom Kippur, the holiest day of the Jewish year, as even the littlest ones struggle to act in accordance with the solemnity of the day. And I love watching them on Purim, when we laugh and dance and give charity and eat jam-filled cookies shaped like three-cornered hats.

This is why I recommend that even people who don't consider themselves religious think about attending services with their families. When you take your children to church, or when you say a prayer before you eat or sleep, or when you celebrate a festival, you are instilling values that will help them determine who they are. And all religions teach children that how they treat others really matters. Donald Trump's apprentices want money and fame. But Jesus's apprentices wanted a life of piety and service. Which apprentices do you think had more inner peace and happier marriages? Which ones helped heal the world more, and brought more joy to the Creator? A rapper impregnates women and leaves them with a couple of bucks, reluctant to marry the mothers of his children. But Abraham remained loyal to Sarah for many decades, even though she was barren and he had no heir. Which of these men would you rather your child look up to? Isn't Christmas not just an excuse to max out the AmEx on presents but a spirit, a state of mind that leads us to embrace and show charity toward the elderly, the infirm, and the unfortunate?

Our traditions should give us a higher sense of reality.

When children commemorate a festival like Chanukah, Easter, or Ramadan, they connect with the theme of the holiday, a unique value that they will internalize. In the case of Chanukah, a Jewish child will begin to think of himself as born to be a light, a source of illumination rather than darkness. At Easter, a Christian child contemplates the sacrifice of Christ, and conditions herself to lead a more selfless life, putting her own ego on the back burner. At Ramadan, a Muslim child thinks of the abnegation of self, the denial of everyday necessity, and fortifies himself for a life of the spirit.

Aren't those the kinds of valuable lessons you hope to impart to your children, the kinds of tools that will help them to navigate the world?

CONCLUSION

Inspiration: The Eternal Flame

Could I climb to the highest place in Athens, I would lift my
voice and proclaim, "Fellow citizens, why do you turn and
scrape every stone to gather wealth, and yet take
so little care of your children to whom
one day you must relinquish it all?"
—Socrates

One of the most moving—and for me one of the
saddest—moments that we filmed for *Shalom in the
Home* happened when we were working with a family being
torn apart by the father's rage. The source of much of this
anger seemed to be his relationship with his own father,
whom he felt had never loved him. So I arranged to have the
two men meet, in the hope of some kind of rapprochement.

As this man's father, an ailing man in his seventies, began
to speak of his own difficult childhood, his own feelings of
abandonment and too little love, I realized one thing:
Dysfunction is becoming the new American heirloom.

A lack of passion characterizes the new American parenting tradition, and so an uninspired life has become our

principal legacy to our children, just as it was our parents' legacy to us.

The parents I see screaming at their children don't mean to hurt them; neither do the ones who hand them over to such substitute parents as coaches and video games. They're scarred people themselves, barely keeping their own heads above water.

But unless something is done, right now, this legacy of pain and insecurity will continue. We will give birth to yet another generation of broken children, just like ourselves, and we will watch as those children grow up into insecure adults, monitoring their bank balances and the neighbors' home improvements with an eagle eye, while their own children founder.

So we find ourselves at a crossroads, and every American parent has a choice to make. We can step aside and let things go the way they've been going, or we can finally decide to plant our children into well-nourished soil that will allow them to put down strong, steady roots.

If we take the time and make the effort to effect this change, the possibilities are quite literally limitless. Because if we put a system in place that allows our children to have a different kind of childhood, a more authentic childhood, one characterized by security and a return to innocence, then our legacy to our children will be nothing less than Paradise. And then it will be our pleasure to watch this generation burst into bloom. We will watch them grow up to become a new category of heroes, men and women with nobility of character, who get married and stay married, who put good works before vanity and their own children before work.

But in order to do this, we must heal ourselves. We must redefine success, so that we can show our children unconditional love, not love that is dependent on the grades they get or the size they wear. We must redefine our leisure time so that it is focused around our children, instead of happening in spite of them. We must search within ourselves for our own true values so that we can convey these things to our children, along with an identity and a sense of purposefulness to match.

Coming to this determination is part of being a parent. When I became rabbi at Oxford, I worked my guts out to make Jewish life at that university come alive. I was fighting a losing battle; religion had been defeated at Oxford in the eighteenth century, with the great Huxley-Wilberforce debate, and yet there I was—a Jew! in a country where Christianity was the state religion, at a college that had made their buildings look like cathedrals to prove that science had indeed vanquished religion—as a religious representative.

Against all odds, we were wildly successful; in a few short years, our organization became the second largest student society on campus, with thousands of members and world-class speakers. But my own family was barely making ends meet. My salary was a pittance, and the expenses were enormous—at our peak, we were even catering, literally, to between four and five hundred students a week. So I called the head of Lubavitch in London, and I said to him, "I cannot continue like this. I am working all day and all night, and yet we don't have a penny in the bank. I have to be paid something I can live on. I am doing all this work, and yet I have no security."

He was sympathetic about our financial difficulties, but it

was what he said next that has stayed with me since: "Shmu-ley, do you think security comes in the form of having money put away for your daughters' weddings? That's not security. *Real* security is knowing where your kids will be in thirty years—and that security you have.

"Your kids are being raised in a religious tradition. They sit down for dinner every Friday night, not just with their mother and father, but with some of the brightest students in the country—some of whom are celebrating the Jewish Sab-bath for the very first time in their lives! Your children see their father inspiring people to become better people; they are absorbing that message, and they are inspired by it every day. In thirty years, you will find your children sitting at their own Shabbos tables. *That's* security."

He was absolutely right. During my stay at Oxford, I had met the kids of some of the most influential and wealthy families in the world; the children of celebrities, billionaires, members of Parliament, prime ministers. But these same powerful, wealthy people were calling me in confidence to find out who their daughter was dating, and whether their son's depression was serious enough to merit withdrawing him from school. These people had all the financial security in the world, but they didn't have their children—so what kind of security did they really have?

In the book of Proverbs, King Solomon says that the child is the arrow, and the parent the bow. I believe that the strength with which we pull back our bows is the inspiration with which we parent. And the only real security I know in this world is the knowledge that you have pulled your bow back with all the passion and effort you can muster, sending that arrow off with enough energy and inspiration to guarantee that it reaches its destination: a healthy and purpose-filled life.

Right now, parents in America are pulling their bows back with so little vigor that the arrows they release soon crash to earth, the way we ourselves came straight down. Unfortunately, this lack of inspiration is not something we can fix after the fact. You have a limited time to transfer the energy that will affect the trajectory of the rest of your children's lives. They are going to grow up, move out, and move on—will you be with them when they do?

I saw firsthand at Oxford how many children grew up utterly unaffected, except in a negative way, by their parents. Thrilled to get out of the house, they abused their new freedoms as if they had just been lying in wait for the opportunity to treat themselves with utter disrespect. None of their parents' energy had been transferred to them—none of their passions, and certainly none of their values.

And that kind of foreshortened trajectory is, quite frankly, something I am simply not willing to accept. Because I know, in my heart of hearts, one thing: *if I fail as a parent, I am a failure*. My success in life will be measured by a single standard, my children's stability and sense of direction, and I am nothing if they do not flourish.

This is true of all of us. I don't care who you are, or whatever else you do in your life. Eleanor Roosevelt said that her children had to make appointments to see FDR when he was in the White House, something that has forever colored my impression of that great man. I know he was saving the world from Hitler. Still, he should have made just a little time to see his kids. In this very important respect—he did not succeed. And his failure is written into his family's history: five children, every one of them divorced.

Please don't tell me that the success of your children is somehow out of your control. At this point, we know what's bad for kids—there can be no further debate. We know that permissive parenting fails. We know that not protecting your children from the corrosive influences in the culture fails. We know that not giving your children enough love or time fails. We know that having a bad marriage and dishonoring your spouse poisons your children. We know that if we fail to provide kids with healthy activities, they will spend their time on unhealthy ones. If we don't teach them to embrace their innate sense of wonder, they're going to become addicted to acquisition, unable to renew themselves. If we don't give them strong, meaningful traditions, they will have no identity and no sense of purpose, cursed instead to wander meaninglessly through life.

Nothing I have written in this book is anything more than plain common sense. So there is really no choice about *what* to do—the only question remaining is whether or not we will do it. Will we effect a program like PLANT, or will we continue to see America's kids disintegrate? Will we bring passion and inspiration to our parenting, or will we watch the arrows we launch plummet to the ground?

I have advised you to do nothing in this book that I do not try to do myself. I don't always do it perfectly, but I devote my best energy to it. Because while I may be prepared to fail in some areas of my life, I am not prepared to fail with my children. In this arena, I will not tolerate anything less than success. I may fall out with friends. Some of my books may sell well, others may sink. I enjoy hosting my television show, but ultimately, it is up to the audience whether it does well or not.

But, as I tell my children, with you, I will not fail. In this, I am unshakable. Hurricanes may come, Abercrombie & Fitch catalogues may come, but I will not be moved. Nothing you can do will undermine my commitment to you, because I have taken a solemn oath on G-d's altar that I will raise good and healthy children.

I am a parent. This is my identity, who I am—a man who has created life in his own image. And while my children will go on to have their own lives, their own interests and passions, my values and the inspiration I have given them will always be at their very center.

Why are Americans the most insecure people in the world? Because we have put our faith in every security but the real one. We insist on seat belts and protection from secondhand smoke; we buy insurance for our cars, for our houses, for our health. President Bush just requested another $72 billion to defend our country against terrorists, and that's important. Yet our most valuable possessions remain unguarded and insecure.

It is in our power to create a new American child, and it is time for us to do so now. We will know this new breed of American, because for them, security will not come merely in the form of a mutual fund portfolio or a 401(k), but from their inner stability and the force of their convictions. Their strength will come from the knowledge that there are things they will never do; their comfort will come from knowing that there are compromises they will never make. And this will be the powerful legacy that they bequeath to their *own* children, an American heirloom that is truly worth transmitting.